Second Edition

Communication Training and Development

William E. Arnold
Lynne McClure

WAVELAND
PRESS, INC.

Prospect Heights, Illinois

For information about this book, write or call:

Waveland Press, Inc.
P.O. Box 400
Prospect Heights, Illinois 60070
(708) 634-0081

Contents

vi   *Contents*

List of Exhibits

Exhibit

Preface

Welcome to the world of training and development (T & D). Whether this is your first visit or you are a regular to training and consulting, we plan to guide you through all the facets of the field. The material for this book has been provided by other writers in the field, as well as from our personal experiences in training and in teaching courses in T & D.

In this second edition we have enhanced the material in each chapter. We have incorporated the suggestions provided by our students and our colleagues. We have upgraded the discussion of technology while recognizing that any information put in print will be outdated by the time it reaches your hands. With that technology explosion in mind, we have focused on broad-based material rather than suggesting which specific software you should use.

T & D is the process through which companies and other organizations help managers and employees improve performance and increase job satisfaction. In training, the improved performance relates specifically to the individual's job skills. An executive assistant, for example, would get training in word-processing skills; an accountant would be trained in new tax laws; and a manager would be trained in performance-appraisal methods. In development, the improved performance relates to broader skills that may do two things: prepare an employee or manager for a position with increased responsibilities; and enhance an individual's personal life as well as his or her work performance. Workshops in communication, individual goal setting, values clarification, career enhancement, management styles, and related topics would help individuals perform better at work, but they also could affect their personal lives and relationships. Training tends to be job specific. Development tends to focus on the individual.

Communication relates to training and development in two ways. First, communication is a field in itself—an area in which all companies and organizations, and employees and managers at all levels, continually need improvement. Engineers, medical and health professionals, accountants, construction workers, secretaries, managers, and attorneys, among others, are skilled in their professions and trades but not in ways to communicate effectively with coworkers, bosses, employees, customers, clients, and associates. Second, communication is the medium through which all other skills and information are delivered. Training and development specialists in all fields need effective communication skills to train employees and to develop their potential. This book addresses both ways communication relates to training and development. It presents training and development skills in the field of communication, and it presents communication skills to use in any area of training and development. Clearly we view training and development and communication as interrelated. Each of the processes that is used in communication training and development can be used in the general field of training and development.

This book is unique in several ways:

- We are both experienced consultants. One of us is a professor of communication who uses his expertise to serve as a consultant to firms and organizations. The other, president of a management consulting firm, has successfully served client companies nationwide since 1980 and was the speaker on videotapes and audiotapes marketed nationally by a New York firm.

- We give specific "how-tos," making the book practical and applicable in its orientation. The "how-tos" are spelled out in a step-by step method, allowing the reader to go beyond "knowing how" and actually carry out these steps.

- We include numerous anecdotes based on our experiences in training and development. These anecdotes serve to make the information relevant and memorable.

- We address the subtle, but often crucial, ways in which office politics affect training and development. We also give practical suggestions about ways to deal with politics.

- We present the information in a style that is lively, conversational, and easy to read.

We wrote this book to fill two big gaps—the practical application of training and development principles in the field of communication, and the practical application of communication principles in the field of training and development. This book is more than just "about" communication or training and development—it shows you how to do it.

To use this book to full advantage, the reader can think of places he or she has worked or groups to which he or she has belonged, and see how the points and skills described in the book would apply. The practical nature of this book makes it applicable to innumerable settings.

The book will benefit university juniors and seniors in communication, management, or adult education. It is a must for training and development classes, and an excellent supplement for management courses and adult education classes. Instructors may want to assign student teams to conduct actual needs assessments—described step-by-step in the book—in local companies and organizations. Or, students could be assigned to present actual workshops—also described in the book—to the class.

So, if you are looking for a history on the progression of the field of training and development, we suggest you consult some of the books and articles highlighted in the bibliography. We decided that a practical, easy-to-read book could make a greater contribution to the development of effective trainers. We hope you will agree with us.

William E. Arnold
Lynne McClure

Introduction

Objectives

This chapter will help you

► understand training and development in the field of communication
► recognize important characteristics of communication
► distinguish between *training* and *development*
► identify ways to use training and development within organizations

Why Is Training and Development a Field of Communication?

If you want a career in training, this book will serve as an introduction to the field. If your career goal is to become a manager, the points discussed in this book will help you develop successful ways of dealing with employees. If you are not yet certain about your career goals, this book will give you ideas to consider. The focus of the book is on the practical application at work of many concepts you learn in college.

The training and development field—T & D—has its own methods, literature, jargon, practitioner journals, societies, research, and folklore, as do all professions. An organization's productivity and success depend a lot on the nature and quality of its T & D. Everything about an employee's behavior—job performance, productivity, morale, turnover, absenteeism, teamwork, dedication, growth, commitment, career development, and related issues—is affected by the company's T & D efforts. Companies of all sizes use internal training, public workshops, outside consultants, traditional and nontraditional college courses, and other resources to train and develop their employees. Many large companies have entire departments responsible for T & D. An organization's T & D program serves as a visible indicator of management philosophy at work.

Whether it is done well or poorly, superficially or thoroughly, some kind of T & D exists in all jobs, companies, and organizations. Because of the variety of types of companies and organizations, T & D takes many forms. Sometimes it is done in a casual, haphazard way; for example, an employee may be expected to figure out the work by watching and listening to others who have the same job. At other times, the T & D may be formal, requiring employees to take courses related to new equipment or procedures. Many companies offer continuing training programs that employees may take voluntarily, and other firms require specific training of their employees. Occasionally, T & D covers personal, as well as work-related, subjects. For example, a workshop dealing with listening skills may include ways to get along at home as well as at work. Companies also may offer courses in such topics as personal finances or physical fitness. Whatever the style, T & D most often focuses on the specific work at hand. In one restaurant, a new server may be told simply to copy what the other servers do. In another restaurant, he or she may go through extensive training that covers serving wine, pronouncing French names, and choosing formal clothes.

When we talk about *communication* training and development, we address the single common thread that crosses boundaries between organizations and job needs: the ability to communicate effectively. According to research findings, a basic communication model is as diagrammed in Exhibit 1.1. The sender is the person speaking or otherwise delivering a message, and the receiver is the person who reads, hears, or otherwise gets the message. Feedback is the receiver's response, which may be in the form of words, facial expressions, or actions. Communication T & D focuses on helping people in organizations learn how to communicate with each other. At first glance, you may be surprised about this need. You may ask, "Why do people have to learn this at work? Don't they already know this?" Unfortunately, the answer is often a resounding "No."

Exhibit 1.1   Basic Communication Model

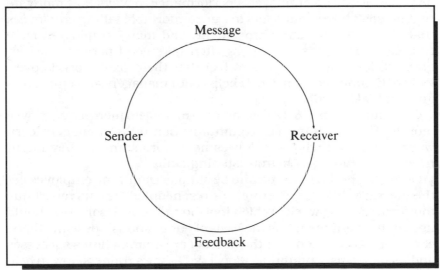

Organizations are fraught with communication problems, which at times deal directly with the work at hand. For example, how do you explain a job clearly and thoroughly without overwhelming a new employee with details? If you focus only on the details of a job, the employee may not understand why certain steps are important. On the other hand, if you give "the big picture" to a new employee too soon, he or she may have trouble understanding the boundaries of the job. As an example, consider the job of cashier. One new cashier may need to learn how to use the computerized cash register before learning anything else. Another new cashier may want to learn about the whole department and its policies before learning details about the computer. Through communication training and development, managers learn how to organize and pace information for new employees.

Managers need to understand various ways different employees learn; for instance, what is the best way to teach someone how to use a complex piece of machinery? Some people want only hands-on experience, while others like to read technical descriptions first.

Another problem is how to define job duties that are not easily measurable. For example, suppose the job of hotel clerk requires that employees behave in a "businesslike manner." One person's definition of "businesslike" may be very different from another's. Managers must be able to translate these kinds of job duties into specific behaviors.

Other times, communication problems involve the future. How do you evaluate an employee's performance in ways that motivate that person? Many managers are uncomfortable telling employees that their work needs improvement, and many employees have trouble hearing this. Managers often take good performance for granted, leading employees to feel that their good work is over-looked. Communication T & D helps both managers and employees give and take feedback.

Communication T & D also can help managers increase employee morale. Through improved communication skills, managers learn ways to find out what employees need; for example, they might need to be trained in better listening skills.

Often, the problems appear to be simple: Didn't the employee get the message that our meeting was rescheduled? Is this report due tomorrow or next week? Which tool did the supervisor say I should use on this equipment? As the basis of our relationships with others, communication often is at the heart of an organization's successes and its problems. Communication T & D shows trainers how to help people communicate more effectively.

What Is Communication?

Communication, like T & D, is a field in itself. This book focuses not on specific communication areas but on *applications* of communication methods, and it presents ways to train individuals and to help them develop their communication skills. Nevertheless, we must start with shared definitions, to be sure we are working toward common goals. Our definitions of communication are listed in the following sections.

What Is Understood Matches What Was Intended

Many people think communication is simply the process of sending out information. Instead, communication is the process of being understood. If the listener understands something different from what is meant, communication has not taken place—*mis*communication has. Effective communication means that what is understood matches what was intended.

Roles, Relationships, and Objectives Are Clear

If communication has taken place, individuals understand what roles they play, how their roles relate to each other's, and what functions everyone serves in the overall organization. "Roles" at work are the jobs people are to perform. The relationships among individuals' roles are important, because each person's job affects others' work. Objectives often become problems at work because so many types and levels of objectives exist. The objectives of the firm, of each department, and of individual employees may differ from or even conflict with each other. Let's use a manufacturing firm as an example. One goal of the marketing department is to sell as much product as it can, while a goal of the production department is to make quality products at low cost. Conflicts between these two departments often arise when marketing says customers want certain changes in the product, but production says the changes would be too costly. To accomplish anything, these different objectives must be worked out and meshed. Because nothing ever stands still, the process of clarifying roles, relationships, and objectives is ongoing.

Thoughts, Feelings, and Attitudes Are Expressed

When group members are open about what they think and feel, the group develops trust, understanding, and the ability to work things out for everyone's benefit. Hiding the inner self—that is, refusing to communicate—works against the effectiveness of groups and relationships. Yet many individuals find it difficult to be honest about what they think or feel. Sometimes they are wise to hold back, because the environment does not allow for openness. For example, do you always tell your best friend only the truth? At work, a manager's gruffness and unapproachable management style may discourage employees from giving honest feedback. Other times, people hold back unnecessarily because of their own personal fears.

The problem is that the success of a group depends on the degree of honesty each member can give and receive. In a group that communicates well, thoughts, feelings, and attitudes are expressed. This is especially true today, because teams and teamwork are more common and more important than ever. Honesty, in a kind manner, is important to successful teamwork.

Specific Wants, Needs, and Instructions Are Identified

In addition to expressing your views honestly, it's also important to specify what you want others to do. Vague descriptions or the hope that others will read your mind are doomed to failure. Many of us, however, operate this way without realizing it. We assume that our own perceptions of the world are self-evident to others, and that therefore others will know exactly what we mean or what we need. This assumption ignores the fact that people have their own sense of reality, and that we all have different ideas about what any situation calls for. Communication involves making your expectations clear to others.

Process, Rather than Content, Is Emphasized

Content means what people say, and *process* means how they say it. Often, the content and process of a statement contradict each other. Suppose a manager says, "I'm interested in hearing about your problem." The content level of this statement is clear. To match the content level, the manager's process would include such nonverbal clues as eye contact with the employee, a friendly and supportive tone of voice, a facial expression that shows concern and interest, and body posture that is open. If, however, the manager's process is abrupt, defensive, angry, or closed, it will contradict the content. Research shows us that most people will believe the nonverbal message more than the verbal.

Very often in organizations and in relationships, people think they disagree in the content area when the problem is, in fact, on the process level. For example, two employees may have a conflict about the best way to get a job done, when the real problem is that their boss encourages competition rather than cooperation. In this case, the best way to get a job done is not really the issue. The issue is that neither employee wants to agree with the other. Process—in this case, the way people relate to others, and what kinds of behaviors are rewarded—must be dealt with before the employees and the company can function well. The focus of communication is on how people relate to each other—what processes, cues, and other forms of interaction occur, and how they affect relationships and productivity—as well as on what is said.

Communication is all of these things and more. Despite what many people assume, and act on, communication does not just happen by itself. Instead, it takes a great deal of conscious effort, practice, and training. The natural order of things leads more often to miscommunication than to good communication. In organizations, nearly every problem can be traced to a communication problem; but this fact only adds to the confusion, because the subject is so broad. Communication T & D helps people at the process level (things they can do to communicate effectively) so they can better convey the content they wish to deliver.

What Is Training and Development?

Although the two words often are used together, and although they both deal with improving human performance, the words "training" and "development" represent two different emphases. Traditionally, training means teaching people things they need to know for their current jobs, while development means preparing them for the future.

Training

Training refers to teaching specific skills to individuals. These skills, required by the present job, include the following:

- physical manipulations, such as running a machine
- specific procedures, such as how to order new materials
- company policy, such as supplying an employee with the name of a manager when a personal problem affects his or her work performance
- specific behaviors, such as how to deal with customers over the telephone
- specific methods, such as how to fill out grant applications

Training can take place anytime during a person's career. A new employee needs training to learn the specifics about the job and company policy. A long-term employee needs to learn how to use the new computer system. Workers need to develop supervisory skills so they can be promoted. New managers need to be trained to deal with specific problems they face in their new jobs. High-level managers need to learn additional skills, such as public speaking or business writing. Teams need team-building and team-maintenance skills. Training is a broad area that covers these and other job-related skills, and takes place on several levels.

Informational level.   The first is the informational level, where the purpose of training is to teach a person *about* something. Company policy, the importance of following procedures, or rules about work are examples of information that can be taught. Even skills, such as how to give effective presentations or how to use a computer, may be taught at the informational level. In these cases, the person learns thoughts and ideas about a topic, but does not have any physical or applied exposure to the topic. The goal of informational training is to increase trainees' awareness of a topic. This book will give you informational training.

Behavioral level.   The second level of training is *behavioral*, which goes beyond thoughts and ideas and gets into specific ways to act or to perform tasks. If the topic were how to give presentations, trainees learning at the behavioral level would actually design, write, and give presentations to the group. If the topic were computers, trainees would actually sit down at computers and design or use programs. The goal of behavioral training is to teach trainees how to do something.

Results-oriented level.   The third level of learning is *results-oriented*, where trainees' learning is designed to have an effect on the organization. For example, managers who learn how to use performance-evaluation sessions as motivators of their employees may help decrease employee turnover in the company. Because organization-wide results are long term rather than immediately noticeable, they often are difficult to measure. Nevertheless, the goal of results-oriented training is to improve the productivity of an organization and to help determine its future.

Whether the training is informational, behavioral, or results-oriented, it relates specifically to job skills employees need in order to do their work. Often, these skills result in effects that are long-range or that go beyond the job. For example, a person may learn how to deal with angry customers (a behavioral skill) and this ability may change the way that person deals with people in the office, at home, and elsewhere. In a sense, the carry-over means that the training has gone in the direction of development, because the training is not limited to the person's present job. Nevertheless, specific information,behaviors, methods, procedures, and physical manipulations comprise training.

Development

The development of a person includes, but does not stop at, training. Development includes more conceptual understanding of the "why," and more cognitive recognition of how certain behaviors or skills fit into the wider context of the entire organization. Development involves a systems approach. In a systems approach, each person's job is seen not only as an activity in itself, but also as one part of the organizational plan. Beginning with self-awareness, individuals learn how they fit into the roles and relationships within the department and, later, within the entire organization. They also learn how others relate to this larger context.

Self-awareness is the key to individual development. Self-awareness begins with a realization of how you come across to others: how they interpret your behavior, regardless of your intentions. Often, people are surprised at the difference between how they see themselves and how others see them. The difference may be positive: others think more favorably about their behavior than the individual had expected, or others benefit more from the individual's behavior than he or she realized. Or the difference may be negative, as when people think they manage in a participative way but their employees see them as narrow-minded dictators. As an example, an executive who was a client of ours had a company-wide reputation for being cold, harsh, unpredictable, and indifferent to employees' needs. He was aware of his reputation, but disagreed with it, believing himself to be very concerned about his employees and methodical in his methods. By disagreeing instead of listening, this executive cut off feedback and opportunities to learn from it.

Others' reactions to you are a form of feedback, telling you how you come across. This kind of feedback is crucial to self-awareness, because it helps you learn what you actually do, how you affect others, and how effectively you carry out your intentions. When the feedback differs from your own expectations, it can help you change your behavior. The feedback may also alert you to unacknowledged needs you have or unacknowledged room for growth. Self-awareness begins the long process of individual development. The Johari Window, developed by Joseph Luft and Harry Ingham, represents various levels of self-awareness. The purpose of the Johari Window is to help individuals identify how much they know about their own behaviors. The "window" looks like the illustration in Exhibit 1.2. Box 1 represents those things about ourselves that we and others know; for example, whether we are tall or short. In terms of our behavior, this area might include such things as our moodiness, our good sense of humor, or the types of people we like to date. Box 2 represents things we know about ourselves but do not share with others. For some people, this area would include their political views, while for others it might be such things as their long-term goals, personal morals, or social lives. Box 3 represents things others know about us but of which we are unaware. For example, your friends, and *not* you, might know that you frown when you read or that you laugh when you are nervous. Box 4 represents a blind spot, where neither you nor others are aware of certain of your behaviors. The Johari Window is not something you would draw literally and carry around with you. Instead, it is a model that can help you become aware of how you act and how you relate to others. As an example, suppose you got along well with all but one person in your social group, whom we'll call John. You could use the Johari Window in the following way:

1. First, in Box 1, identify what you share with John: what is known to him and to you about how you act toward him. This is a way of asking yourself how you look from John's point of view.

Exhibit 1.2   The Johari Window

	Known to Others	Unknown to Others
Known to Self	1	2
Unknown to Self	3	4

2. Second, in Box 2, identify what you keep from John: what you know or do that John is unaware of. This is a way of finding out what John may not know about you. Would you get along any better with him if he knew some of this about you?
3. Third, in Box 3, put yourself in John's place and try to imagine what he may know, see, or think about you that you are unaware of. Could your unawareness be hurting the relationship? Might John misunderstand you?
4. Fourth, the blind spot in Box 4 is not relevant because it involves issues that neither you nor John is aware of. So, based on your analysis of the first three boxes, are there things you could do to improve the relationship with John?

After a while, you may begin thinking this way automatically. The Johari Window is a useful model for increasing your self-awareness.

The process of self-awareness is continuing and disjointed. It occurs in large and small pieces and in unpredictable time frames. Moments of self-realization may take place spontaneously, often days, weeks, or months after a planned development activity. Because of the disorganized nature of individual development, the steps overlap instead of following a sequence.

Roles

Once self-awareness begins, you are ready to learn more about the ways people relate to each other. One aspect of relationships at work involves roles people play. A *functional role* is a summary of your job description: what you are responsible for at work. For example, an office manager's functional role is to make sure the office runs smoothly; the functional role of an ironworker is to build a solid framework for a building. The *behavioral role* you play involves the ways you interact with other people. It is predictable, consistent behavior that, over time, others come to expect from you. Your behavioral role has nothing to do with your intentions—that is, what you think you are doing. Instead, your behavioral role is what you actually do, and how your actions affect others. As an example, every office has someone whose behavioral role is the complainer—someone who will object no matter what the circumstances are. Other examples of common behavioral roles at work are the worrier, who predicts gloom and doom for any project; the optimist, who sees the good side despite bad news; the early bird, who considers a person late when that person is on time; and the gossip, who knows and spreads personal news about colleagues. All of us have behavioral roles that describe our ways of interacting with others. Benne and Sheats (1948) identify the following categories of roles:

- **Group Task Roles**

  Initiator-contributor: starts discussions and begins changes
  Information seeker: asks for clarification of facts
  Opinion seeker: asks to clarify group's values
  Information giver: offers "authoritative" information
  Opinion giver: influences group's values
  Elaborator: uses examples, presents implications
  Coordinator: pulls ideas together
  Orienter: summarizes what has gone on in discussion
  Evaluator-critic: sets standards for group
  Energizer: prods group into action
  Procedural-technician: does tasks for the group
  Recorder: keeps written records

- **Group Building and Maintenance Roles**

  Encourager: offers praise and warmth within group
  Harmonizer: mediates differences among members
  Compromiser: tries to establish agreement in group
  Gate-keeper: encourages participation from all
  Standard-setter: uses standards to guide group action
  Group-observer: interprets group processes
  Follower: passively goes along with group

- **Individual Roles**

  Aggressor: "attacks" group in various ways
  Blocker: negatively resists group processes
  Recognition-seeker: calls attention to self
  Self-confessor: expresses nongroup-oriented ideas
  Playboy-playgirl: flaunts a lack of involvement
  Dominator: uses manipulation to gain authority
  Help-seeker: seeks sympathy from group
  Special-interest pleader: disguises own biases through representing special groups

Interestingly, our functional roles and behavioral roles do not necessarily predict each other. An employee may behave more like a leader than the manager does. A supervisor with a great deal of responsibility may act out the behavioral role of the forgetful one. In the area of individual development, behavioral roles are more important than functional roles. Behavioral roles describe our predictable behaviors, as others have come to expect from us. When we get feedback from others, we learn their perceptions of the behavioral roles we play. To repeat, we may be surprised when people describe us in terms of behavioral roles we did not realize we were playing. The surprise comes from the fact that our intentions often are different from the way our behaviors come across.

Recognition of our behavioral roles is crucial to development. Social learning theory (Bandura, 1977) describes the interaction among individuals, their behaviors, and their environments: all three affect each other equally. According to part of this theory, one's behavior draws reactions from others and these reactions become part of one's environment. That is, the ways others respond become part of one's surroundings—an atmosphere of praise, criticism, encouragement, resentment, support, or an infinite number of other possibilities. For example, a manager may have a policy of praising employees whenever they suggest money-saving ideas. This manager's response—praise—becomes part of the employees' environment. In turn, the environment affects them and thus influences the way they behave. Because they know, for example, that the manager praises money-saving ideas, the employees are likely to come up with these ideas frequently. Based on this part of social learning theory, the predictable nature of our behavioral roles draws predictable reactions from others. Getting to know people means becoming able to predict their behavioral roles; and as others' behaviors become predictable to us, our behaviors in turn become familiar to them. The interaction among behavioral roles— each person's behavior drawing predictable reactions from the others—means that we may influence others' actions. Once we know the behavioral roles we tend to act out, we can better understand why people respond to us the way they do.

For example, an employee we'll call Susan has had her job for six months. Susan's boss has told her that her work is fine, so Susan feels comfortable about her ability to perform well on the job. However, she has noticed that on a social level, she has problems with several coworkers. Realizing that the informal system—that is, the social side—at work could affect her job security, Susan decides to analyze her interaction with her coworkers. Looking first at her own behaviors, Susan recognizes that her behavior at work includes reminding others about their deadlines. Susan means well; that is, her coworkers' deadlines affect her own work, and her intention is to be helpful to them as well. In terms of her behavior, however, Susan realizes that she acts out the role of the "office nag." Her behavioral role creates resentment among her coworkers because they perceive her as not giving them credit for managing their own work loads or schedules. Because of her behavioral role, and her coworkers' resentment of this role, Susan has unwittingly invited negative reactions from others, which she did not intend.

Once she realizes how her own behaviors draw negative behaviors from her coworkers, Susan is able to change the relationships. She watches her own work and time frames, and deals with her peers in the usual way except for one thing: she no longer refers to their deadlines. Instead, she leaves their time management up to them. At first, no one notices, because their expectations already have been established and people continue to perceive Susan in terms of her familiar behavioral role. Over time, however, her coworkers come to realize that Susan no longer nags them, and they begin reacting to her in a more relaxed way. Within a month, the relationships among Susan and her peers are much friendlier and more open than before. In terms of predictable roles, Susan's change in behavior brings about different and more positive responses from her coworkers.

This example shows how we can affect the way people respond to us, by recognizing and modifying our own predictable behavioral roles. Development includes this self-awareness and recognition of our behaviors.

In development, an individual also would learn how these behaviors fit into the broader picture: company needs, his or her own interests and goals, and other opportunities within the firm. Development increases individuals' self-awareness, helping them discover how they relate to others, how their self-images compare to others' perceptions of them, and what their strengths and weaknesses are. Development also deals with individuals' long-term career goals, first by helping people learn what their skills, interests, and capabilities are. The next step is to help them identify their specific goals. For example, someone who is good in math may want to go into accounting, computer programming, engineering, or any number of other careers. Once the specific goal is identified by the manager and worker, the next step is to help individuals identify the training they need to reach these goals. Some people may want to go to college or enroll in graduate programs, while others need in-house courses or outside workshops. While training focuses on specific skills and behaviors, development aims at helping people achieve their full potential, both personally and professionally.

Training and development, as a field, emphasizes two different sides of one process. When the emphasis is development, the newly learned skills and behaviors affect individuals' self-images, capabilities, and goals. When the emphasis is training, the person must learn specific behaviors and skills to do his or her job well.

Who Needs Communication Training and Development?

Everyone needs communication training and development. In all companies, nonprofit agencies, and other organizations, some people almost always are teaching others how to do the work, how to hire new employees, how to train new workers, how to improve work performance, how to give job evaluations, how to write memos, how to write proposals and reports, how to motivate others, how to get more productivity out of employees, how to deal with customers, how to get help for troubled workers, how to avoid or resolve conflicts, and an infinite number of other issues. Ironically, while many people may be qualified to teach the content of these issues, they are not necessarily skilled in the process of teaching them. The result often is poor learning and, therefore, poor performance due to ineffective communication.

Naturally, the first group of people who should learn communication training and development are those who hope to become trainers: the professionals whose work it is to teach employees within organizations. Sometimes, trainers learn about equipment, company policy, ways to discipline employees, and other content areas they will teach, without learning the processes of training. Partly because communication is a subject area in its own right, and mostly because communication is the system that helps or hinders organizations, all trainers need communication training and development. Another, larger group also needs communication T & D: the managers and supervisors who run organizations. They need to understand and know how to use the communication process, because they are the ones who determine the effectiveness of the company. It is from managers and supervisors that employees—and the managers themselves—learn "how we do things around here": how we make decisions, what kinds of behaviors gain recognition, what it takes to get promoted, how teams can be effective, what quality of performance is expected, what the firm's philosophy is, and numerous other subtleties. Managers and supervisors are also the ones who teach employees how to do specific jobs. Because communication is the basis of everything that goes on among people, everyone who teaches people needs to know how to communicate effectively.

A third group needing communication T & D is the employees themselves. In addition to teaching specific skills to each other, employees continually interact because their work overlaps. Misunderstandings, mistakes, physical dangers, poor work, hard feelings, high costs, and other negatives can result when coworkers have trouble communicating with each other. Working in teams requires constant communication. In addition, employees often feel frustrated because they would like to convey certain ideas to management but they do not feel comfortable doing so, usually because they do not know how. Communication T & D helps employees and, through them, the entire organization.

In fact, there is hardly anyone who does *not* need communication T & D. All of us have multiple roles, and all of us communicate with others in various ways and for various purposes. We all learn from one another. Each of us is a product of our relationships, as well as of our uniqueness. We affect each other, for better or for worse. Because our relationships depend on how well we communicate, we all need training and development.

Summary

Training and development is vital to all organizations. Training relates to employees' specific needs for their current jobs, while development involves a system-wide approach to meeting individual career needs and organizational management needs. Communication training and development teaches trainers how to help people communicate more effectively. Because communication is such a crucial element in organizations, communication T & D serves an important function.

Developing a Background in Training

Objectives

This chapter will help you

- ► enhance communication skills
- ► recognize effective teaching skills
- ► understand data-gathering skills
- ► identify the importance of political skills

Introduction

An adage in the field of communication training and development says that people major in their weaknesses: dentists have tooth problems; managers have trouble organizing their work; and marriage counselors have problems at home. To prevent this folklore from becoming reality, people in communication T & D must excel in what they teach.

Communication Skills

Communication T & D requires individuals who are strong in a number of areas. First, trainers must themselves learn communication skills. To teach these skills, you must do them well yourself.

Supportive Approach

A supportive approach means you are able to show others that you back them, that you want to help them, and that they can trust you. This approach is crucial in communication T & D. Many times, your first task is to gather information and try to identify areas in which people need training. It is important to recognize the potential threat others may feel because you are assessing their needs. This reaction may surprise you, unless you realize what others' perceptions are. They may be afraid that you will think negatively of them, that their lack of knowledge will get them in trouble, or that you are "spying" for "the bosses." From their point of view, you are an "outsider" who is asking questions about their weaknesses. Remember that you literally *are* an outsider if you are an external consultant. Even if you work for the same organization, you still are an outsider to their department. As an insider, you also may be perceived as capable of harming their careers. People naturally resist opening up when they have such perceptions.

To overcome their fears, you must indicate support. This approach begins in your everyday relationships with people. Your continuing relationships—that is, your reputation—must be characterized by honesty, consideration, discretion, and confidentiality. You must not have a reputation for being thoughtless or gossipy if you expect people to relax when you ask questions about their work. Your day-to-day interactions with others will determine how much confidence they have in you. To prevent people from becoming fearful or suspicious when you try to help them, your general behavior must match your supportive role. For example, one of the authors was interviewing employees as part of the preparation for a workshop. One of the employees (we'll call her Ellen) appeared extremely shy and nervous. Instead of ignoring her behavior or dwelling on it, the interviewer said, "It's natural to be a little unsure about all this. Let me start by describing the purposes of these interviews and how we assure confidentiality." Ellen became more relaxed and willingly shared her views because of the interviewer's supportive style.

Once you have established a supportive reputation, people will more likely feel comfortable talking to you about their training needs. During these conversations, you must maintain your supportive role; you should be an empathic listener—that is, one who can identify with the speaker's feelings and needs.

Accept, rather than judge, people. While you are evaluating performance skills in order to identify training needs, you are not evaluating the individual. The way to clarify what you are evaluating is to focus on behaviors, rather than on an employee's intentions or attitudes. For example, suppose Joe Smith, a mechanic in your firm, has become a supervisor. Your job is to find out how much Joe already knows about supervision and what information or experience he needs to become effective in his new role. Your job is not to determine whether he should have been promoted, whether he has the proper attitude to be a supervisor, or other relatively personal issues.

Another way to maintain your supportive role is to view, and help the trainees view, learning as a growth process. Too often, employees fear that the need for training means they have some kind of "fault" or shortcoming. As a communication T & D specialist, your job includes making trainees feel comfortable about the fact that learning is a lifelong process.

Through a supportive approach, then, you will enhance your communication skills and help employees to perform better at their jobs.

Active Listening

Do you listen to what people say, instead of thinking of your responses while others talk? Do you ask clarifying questions when you do not understand? Do you paraphrase what people say to you, to make sure you get the full impact? Perhaps even more important, do you hear beyond the words and recognize other people's feelings or states of mind? One of the hardest things about listening actively is that we often get too involved with our own feelings or ideas. Because of our selective perception, we risk hearing what we expect, or want, to hear the other person say.

Good listening is necessary for several reasons. First, we need to separate the symptom—that is, behavior we do not like—from the problem; that is, the meaning behind the behavior. We cannot make the separation without excellent listening skills. Symptoms are often mistakenly identified as the problem. For example, in an office where employees do not get along well, the manager may think the problem is one or more of the personalities involved, when the actual problem is lack of job descriptions. Joe and Susan may each think the other should file the daily reports; the result may be that none of the reports gets filed, or that Joe and Susan continually argue about who should do it. In this case, personality conflicts are *symptoms* of the problem, but the lack of clarity about responsibilities is the underlying cause. It takes good listening skills to get past the symptoms and identify the actual problems.

Second, listening skills are important because communication T & D people are responsible for identifying individuals' needs. These needs may be relatively easy to pick out, such as learning how to use a new computer system, or relatively complicated, such as planning the development of a career. Communication T & D people have found that most people cannot clearly specify what their needs are. Most of us deal with symptoms (we are unhappy; we feel frustrated) but do not immediately recognize what needs these symptoms reflect. T & D specialists must listen well to help others identify their needs. Closely related to this skill is the ability to identify resources available to employees, and to help match individuals with these resources.

As an example of needs and resources, an employee may want to learn how to write technical reports. In this case, the firm could provide writing workshops during working hours. A more difficult situation occurs when an employee's work suddenly deteriorates. While the work performance may clearly be declining, the *cause*— that is, what the employee needs—is not so easy to identify. Is the employee responsible for new tasks, in which case he or she needs to learn new work skills? Did management do something that the employee resents, in which case feedback is required? Does the employee have personal problems that require professional counseling? Active listening is required before the trainer can find out what the employee's real needs are.

A third reason for good listening skills is that communication T & D specialists provide opportunities for personal and professional growth within organizations. Employees may want help identifying potential career paths within the firm. This involves learning about the organization's long-term plans, current or potential positions available, and steps employees might take to qualify for these positions. Many companies pay all or part of employees' educational expenses, or send employees to professional workshops and seminars. Often, the topics covered are not limited to work-related issues and expand into areas of personal growth. T & D specialists need effective listening skills to identify individuals' growth needs and appropriate training resources within the community.

In many ways, the communication T & D function is that of liaison, because the T & D person conveys to upper management the needs or wishes of managers, supervisors, and workers on other levels. In addition to conveying information, the T & D specialist often is in a position to influence upper management—that is, to convince them that growth opportunities for employees are worth the time and money they will cost. (This responsibility is discussed in more detail in chapter 5.)

The T & D individual must be a good listener in order to identify applicable needs, to accurately discern the problems involved, and to help resolve potential conflicts. Through active listening, trainers are able to get outside themselves to identify and meet others' needs.

Positive and Constructive Feedback

Feedback means a response to what someone does or says. It is our reaction to their behavior. In many ways, our feedback—that is, how we react to others—affects their behavior. In a work situation, managers can unknowingly discourage employees by giving inappropriate feedback. For example, employees who complain "My boss always tells me when I've done something wrong, but never says how I could improve" are asking for specific suggestions about desired performance. Specialists in communication T & D help managers recognize types of feedback that encourage, instead of discourage, employees. T & D people help managers with both content (what they talk about) and process (how they say it).

To help employees learn and grow, managers must give them "reality checks"—that is, honest, sympathetic responses to what they do. Is the performance excellent? Managers must say so, because recognition is the best reward there is. Is the performance acceptable? Employees need to know both what they do well and in what ways they could improve. Is the performance poor? Managers must tell them, so they can learn. One manager for whom we have consulted was well liked and respected by her employees. Jean not only gave praise on a regular basis, but when employees made mistakes, she had a special way of giving them feedback. Instead of saying they had done something wrong, Jean would say, "Here is a way to make this even better." Her positive emphasis encouraged her employees. The trainer's job is to help managers give effective feedback to employees.

In all these cases, your feedback should focus on behaviors (what people *do*) instead of on personalities or intentions. Through emphasizing behaviors, you avoid hurt feelings and increase your professionalism.

Congruence Between Verbal and Nonverbal Behavior

Look and act the way you sound. People will not trust you if your words are soothing and friendly but your arms are crossed in front of you and your eyes are averted. When your body language matches your words, people are more likely to believe you. Your dress, posture, tone of voice, facial expressions, and general appearance are extensions of body language. Do you *look* like a professional?

Throughout organizations, people often need help in how they behave. Most managers' training does not include specific ways to create congruence, or agreement, in their verbal and nonverbal messages. The result often is misunderstanding between managers and their employees. Communication T & D specialists help bridge this gap through training programs. Again, you must exhibit this agreement yourself if you are to help others do so.

Responsibility for Your Feelings

Use "I" phrases to state how you feel. "I get upset when you do that" is more mature and less accusatory than "You make me upset when you do that." After all, do you really give others the power to make you feel certain ways, or do you acknowledge that your feelings are your own? Many problems in organizations stem from the fact that people project their feelings onto others, instead of recognizing that their feelings are their own. By taking responsibility for your feelings, you let others learn about you. Communication T & D people help others express themselves in nondefensive, nonthreatening ways. They set the example by their own behavior.

A supportive approach, active listening, positive feedback, and congruent messages are the communication skills that are most important if you want to be effective and be taken seriously as a communication T & D specialist.

Teaching Skills

Being a good communicator is necessary, but it is not enough. Communication T & D requires that you understand adult learners and use effective teaching methods. A discussion of the skills important for effective training and development in organizations follows.

Organizational Ability

Good teaching means preparing ahead and being flexible when unanticipated questions or situations come up. Do you have clear objectives of your own for each training session? Are your objectives clear to, and compatible with, those of the group? Do you know how much time each topic requires? Do you have small-group discussions, role-plays, and interactive activities planned? What questions may come up? What problems could occur?

In a work setting, "canned" programs (where the content is fixed, regardless of the needs of each group) can have negative results. You need to be flexible enough to vary the emphasis and the content of each program according to each group's needs. You also need to know your content material very well, in order to be as flexible as you'll need to be.

Awareness of Adult Learners' Needs

It is important to know that because work environments involve adults, effective trainers must recognize that adults learn in ways that are different from younger students. Therefore, one of the teaching skills trainers need is the ability to work with adult learners. Chapter 3 will discuss the specific needs of adult and other nontraditional learners.

Facilitative Style

Many diverse teaching methods are available to trainers. In general, however, an effective trainer is more *facilitator*—one who leads and guides the program—than instructor—one who simply delivers expertise. The facilitative style may be carried out in a number of active and interactive ways: large- and small-group discussions, simulations, and self-awareness exercises.

Large-group discussions. At work, employees and managers can deal with large groups, such as interdepartmental meetings and committees. In large-group discussions, the trainer facilitates by asking questions, tying together comments made by individual participants, and generally getting input from a number of people. These discussions enable participants to give their own examples, ask questions, share their experiences, and feel involved.

In large-group discussions, the trainer must make sure everyone has a chance to participate. Some individuals may need encouragement to talk, while others may need to talk less. Still others may want only to listen, and they must be made to feel that their comments are welcome but not compulsory. The trainer's role is to help everyone feel comfortable and to make sense of what everyone says by summarizing and by grouping related ideas. At the same time, the trainer is the most knowledgeable member of the group. The trainer is the one responsible for making sure the objectives—what everyone is to learn—are met.

Small-group discussions. At work, small groups consist of co-workers who are involved in projects, committees and teams. In small-group discussion, two to six participants discuss issues among themselves with a facilitator. Through this method, everyone has a chance to speak up without being intimidated by the larger group. Usually, each small group has a representative who presents the small group's ideas to the larger group.

Again, the trainer's role is to make sure everyone feels comfortable about talking. While no one should ever be pressured to speak, small-group discussions usually allow even the most timid to contribute. Once small groups have discussed an issue, the trainer helps representatives summarize these issues for the large group. The trainer's responsibilities, once again, are to connect the ideas and help participants gain meaning and insight from them.

Simulations. In a simulation, trainees get a chance to practice new skills as if they were in a work situation. Recall that in a lecture, trainees simply listen to information, and in group discussions they add their input to the trainer's information. In a simulation, trainees actually try out what they have learned. Along with practice and experience, they also get feedback—that is, comments about what they have done well and how they could improve. By acting out new skills in a simulation, trainees get a practice run before they apply these skills in the actual situation.

Simulation exercises take several forms. One is *role-plays*, in which two or more trainees interact. For example, suppose the purpose of the training session is to help new supervisors interview potential employees. In a role-play, trainees would practice the interview techniques they have learned. One trainee would play the role of the applicant, and another that of the supervisor. When the mock interview is over, the other trainees give feedback to the supervisor, based on the techniques and methods covered during the session. Particularly when the group is small, every participant may have a chance to act the supervisor's role. But even when only a few play supervisor, all participants benefit because they learn from watching each other and from giving feedback.

Another simulation is the *in-basket exercise*: one trainee at a time deals with events or situations that could occur on the job. For example, the training session may be about the flow of information within an organization. An in-basket exercise might consist of a number of requests for information about which the trainee has to make decisions. What is the order of priority of these requests? Which requests should be handled by another department? What is the proper way to deny inappropriate requests? Usually, in-basket exercises are done individually, and the trainer gives feedback to the trainee.

Simulations may be designed to match the unique work setting of each trainee or group of trainees. The advantage of simulations is that they give participants a way to practice what they learn, and they provide for feedback about trainees' behavior.

Self-awareness exercises. These exercises take many forms. Most of them, however, are paper-and-pencil questionnaires designed by psychologists, counselors, consultants, teachers, and other professionals. Trainees are instructed to answer the questions as honestly as possible. Based on interpretations prepared by the professionals, the trainer describes to trainees the meanings of their answers. For example, a self-awareness exercise may give the trainees information about how assertive, aggressive, or timid they are. Depending on the results, trainees may want to develop skills in certain areas where they feel they need and want to improve.

The key to self-awareness exercises is that the trainee gets feedback about his or her self-image. It is important to recognize, however, that no self-awareness instrument is foolproof. First, it can be useful only if the trainee's answers are open and accurate.

Second, the wording of the questions may be misleading or, at best, open to interpretation. Third, no instrument can measure all of a person. The best a self-awareness instrument can do is to describe general tendencies of an individual. Each individual must decide how useful this information is. The trainer's role is to help individuals identify their needs and to provide resources to meet these needs.

All of these teaching skills contribute to a trainer's effectiveness.

Data-Gathering Skills

In addition to effective communication and teaching skills, trainers need data-gathering skills. Data gathering, in this context, means finding out what training needs an organization has, a process crucial to successful training. A training program without accurate data gathering is like a medical operation without a diagnosis: potentially dangerous. Trainers use various methods to gather data.

Needs Assessment

A needs assessment is a step-by-step process through which the trainer learns what training must be implemented in an organization.

Why is it so hard to find out about training needs? Aren't they self-evident? The answer is that training needs are expressed in ambiguous, indirect ways. For example, suppose an employee named John has been on the job for two months and his performance ranges from poor to average. We are tempted to say that John's mediocre performance means he does not know how to do the job. However, it also could mean any number of other things, such as:

1. John's supervisor does not know how to give instructions effectively.
2. John's coworkers do not know how to do their jobs, and their inefficiency hurts John's performance.
3. The company's standards are not effectively communicated to employees.

Many other possible explanations of John's performance exist. Needs-assessment skills are required so that the trainer can find out which is the real training need.

The specific steps in needs analysis are discussed in chapter 4.

Task Analysis

In a task analysis, the step-by-step components, or content, of a job are identified. The purpose of a task analysis is to find out what, specifically, a person must know and what he or she must be able to do in order to perform the job well, and then to devise a training program to fit that need.

Job descriptions give an overview of individual jobs. Most job descriptions, however, include only general duties and responsibilities. They usually do not state exactly what skills or behaviors an employee must have to do the job well. For example, the job description for a receptionist's position may read that the receptionist must be friendly. The word "friendly" is too vague, because everyone has a different idea of what it means. To one person, friendly means not being directly critical. To another, it means starting a conversation. To a third, it means sharing personal information. A more accurate job description would specify exactly which behaviors are meant by friendly: frequent eye contact, smiling, relaxed body language, and so forth. Because most job descriptions do not include these specific behaviors, task analysis by an effective trainer identifies exactly what an employee does on the job.

Interviews

As with most of the work trainers do, the data-gathering process involves direct contact with people. A primary method of data gathering is the one-on-one interview, in which the trainer talks with employees to learn their perceptions of training needs.

In most cases, the trainer will not interview all employees because this would be too costly in terms of time and money. Usually, employees are chosen to be interviewed on the basis of random selection. A specific problem, however, sometimes requires interviewing all employees within a particular department, branch office, or other subgroup within the organization.

To interview effectively, the trainer must use all the skills already described to create an atmosphere in which the interviewee will feel comfortable. The employee's comfort level is a major issue in the usefulness of interviews. If employees do not feel confident that they can trust the trainer, they are not likely to give that person candid information.

In addition, the trainer must be skilled in asking the right questions. Suppose, for example, that a company wanted to find out how many employees would sign up for job-related classes at a local university if the firm paid for tuition and books. In this case, the appropriate questions would be relatively specific and straight-forward: "Would you take classes if the company paid for them?" Or, "If so, which classes would interest you?" These kinds of questions call for "yes-no" or equally specific answers.

Suppose, however, that the company wanted information that was much less structured. For example, a firm might want to find out how employees felt about job-related education. Rather than ask questions that called for "yes-no" kinds of answers, the trainer in this case would use questions that called for more individual input from employees. Open-ended questions might be "How much responsibility do you think the company should take for employee education, and how much should employees take?" Or, "What do you think the firm's philosophy about employee education is, and what do you think it should be?" These open-ended questions elicit from employees those issues that are most important to them.

Therefore, if the firm wants to learn which issues are of concern to employees, open-ended questions are most useful. However, if the firm wants specific feedback about a particular topic, "yes-no" questions are most appropriate. The trainer's responsibility is to make certain that the types of questions asked are appropriate to the purpose of the interviews.

Surveys

Another form of data gathering is the written survey, in which all employees anonymously answer questions about the organization. As in the interview method, the key here is the appropriateness of the questions. While open-ended questions are possible in written surveys, the most common are "yes-no" questions or those that require employees to rate items on three-, five-, or ten-point scales.

In many cases, trainers design the survey instruments. In addition to the types of answers called for by the questions, the trainer must consider the relevance of the questions themselves. What if a survey asked employees about five issues that manage-ment considered important, but failed to address issues that employees thought important. This issue of relevance is called *validity*, and trainers must make certain their survey instruments are as valid as possible.

Another consideration is the readability of the questions them-selves. If a trainer is too familiar with his or her intended meanings, there is some risk that the questions may not be as clear as the trainer thinks they are.

In designing and using surveys, trainers must recognize that written instruments lack the interaction that exists in the interview method. Trainers must compensate for this limitation by making surveys valid and by writing them clearly.

Data Analysis

Once data are gathered, they need to be analyzed to be useful. Data analysis is the process of interpreting information to identify what it means about an organization. Statistical analysis is a form of data analysis that deals with quantitative (i.e., numerical) information. Statistical analysis helps determine what issues are most important to employees, the degree of importance of each issue, the relative costs of problems and solutions, how an organization stands compared to its competitors, and a number of other items. Statistical analysis also helps determine whether improvements following a training program are due to the program or to chance. While trainers do not need to be statisticians, they do have to understand enough about data analysis to evaluate and interpret the information they gather.

Data-gathering skills provide trainers with real information about problems, so trainers can design programs that contribute effectively to solutions, and evaluate their programs once they are in operation.

Technological Skills

Trainers often teach various kinds of technological skills: computer programming, computer operating, reading blueprints, writing technical reports, operating a forklift, designing microchips, repairing equipment, splicing genes, and a host of other skills. As you can see, the range is incredibly wide.

No one trainer can perform or teach all of these skills. In this sense, the ability to train is not generic; that is, having good training skills does not mean you can teach anything. At the same time, being good in a technological field does not mean you can teach it. In technological areas, a trainer must first be an expert in the field and, second, must have effective training skills

Political Skills

Organizational politics present many challenges to trainers. Often, these challenges are overlooked or misunderstood, and they can hurt the trainer who is unaware of them.

The issue of politics within an organization can evoke negative reactions from people. To keep the topic as neutral, but as realistic, as possible, we will define *politics* as the *continuing process of negotiating relationships*, but not meaning special favoritism based on personal relationships.

According to our definition, professional and organizational relationships, as with other relationships, are dynamic, constantly evolving processes rather than static events. Subtle shifts, nuances, personal growth, and other issues continually affect our relationships at work. As each person and situation changes, we renegotiate how we will relate to each other. This negotiation does not take place in a formal way; instead, it happens in the ways we behave toward each other.

As an example, suppose Joe is a new employee in a department where everyone else has been employed for three or more years. Over time, this department already has developed its own norms, or ways of behaving. Everyone knows John does not want to chat on Monday mornings; Susan always shows up early; Mary is likely to be late finishing her work; and so on. Relationships have been established over time. As a newcomer, Joe has to find ways to fit in, to identify those behaviors that will help him get along with his coworkers, and to help his coworkers find ways to behave toward him. His presence in the established group creates changes in the group's dynamics. Because each person has to be considered, and because Joe's behavior affects that of others, the group renegotiates relationships or, more simply, finds new ways to relate to each other. Again, these changes may be very subtle, but they still exist.

On a larger scale, organizational politics takes into account that everyone within the organization affects everyone else, and that these relationships are always changing. Within this context, issues of power—the ability to make decisions and carry them out—become crucial. For example, budgetary constraints dictate that certain programs will be funded while others will not. Often, decisions about which projects to fund and which to eliminate depend more on politics than on the objective value of any particular program. While many programs may be valuable objectively, only one or two can be funded. Again, the relationships involved, the politics, may influence these decisions.

The issue of politics is crucial to trainers because in many companies and agencies, training departments are weak politically. Sometimes, the entire training function—not just a specific program—is downsized or even eliminated. It is naive to think that the value of training will speak for itself. With many departments competing for limited budgets, trainers must be able to use the existing political system to make sure their role and function get fair consideration. The objective is to attract support from top management by *emphasizing the value-added*, or *bottom-line improvement*, that training contributes to the firm. Trainers need to earn and maintain the support of top management—as well as the support of the other levels and of teams—if the training role is to survive. Even when the training function is valued, trainers need support from all levels, including top management, before they will be able to gather the data they need to develop training programs. Trainers, therefore, need a certain amount of political astuteness before they can be effective.

Cultural Diversity Skills

Trainers must communicate, assess, teach, and behave in ways to which all company employees can relate. And today's work force is diverse in many ways: for example, race, religion, age, gender, nationality, ethnic background, language, cultural background, values, life-styles, goals, and expertise.

In its broadest sense, diversity means that *everyone* has his or her own needs and ways of learning. No trainer automatically knows how to deal with everyone. He or she can learn, but only by being flexible, curious, observant, and adaptable.

Content Versus Process Skills

In the data-gathering process, trainers must be careful to separate the content and process sides of the messages they deliver and receive. As a reminder, *content* refers to what people say, and *process* refers to how they say it. Often, the process conveys more meaningful information than the content.

For example, a secretary may complain that the boss "never gives me enough information to get the job done right the first time." If you considered only the content of this message, you might assume that the boss needed help to delegate responsibilities. However, suppose that while the secretary talked to you, you noticed a tendency on his or her part to interrupt, finish your sentences for you, and ignore your questions. By observing this process of communicating, you might assume that the secretary needed help with listening skills.

To gather relevant and effective data, the trainer must be skilled at identifying both the content and the process of messages.

Keen Observation

On the process level, people often communicate subtly and indirectly. The effective trainer will notice cues, nuances, hesitations, eagerness, and signals others give. By observing, the trainer often learns when to change the topic, when to pursue a subject in greater depth, and when he or she is coming across well.

Writing Skills

Trainers must write proposals, reports of results, materials to be used in training, and other items. The effectiveness of their ideas and programs often depends on how well they write, in addition to how well they present themselves. Trainers' writing skills, as well as their speaking skills, are important.

Content Specialties

The trainer must be a specialist in communication. Trainers should excel in interpersonal skills, interviewing, group decision making, and a number of other areas. They must also be able to apply their knowledge and experience to work situations, and to convey their information in ways employees can understand and use.

Big Picture Versus Details

The trainer must maintain two views at the same time. The first view is the big picture, the organization as a whole; the second is the detailed view, in which the trainer sees how each individual fits into the big picture. The ability to take an overview and then analyze its details enables the trainer to teach others to the benefit of both individuals and the organization.

Summary

To develop a background in training, trainers need to become familiar with a number of skills. *Communication skills* include a supportive approach, active listening, positive and constructive feedback, congruence between verbal and nonverbal behavior, and responsibility for feelings.

   Teaching skills include organizational skills, awareness of adult learners' needs, facilitative ability, and the ability to conduct large-

and small-group discussions, simulations, and self-awareness exercises. Effective trainers also have the *data-gathering skills* of needs assessments, task analysis, interviews, surveys, and data analysis.

Technological skills, political skills, and *cultural diversity skills* enhance the trainer's ability to have impact on the organization. *Content versus process skills* include observation, writing, content specialties, and big picture versus details.

Because life is a continuous learning process, remember that no one starts out completely knowledgeable about T & D; we all learn as we work. What is important is that we start out with a clear understanding of what we need to learn.

Adult Learning

Objectives

This chapter will help you

- ► understand the principles of adult learning
- ► recognize what motivates adult learners
- ► identify key learning principles for all learners
- ► understand the application of training to adults

Introduction

If you are reading this book as an assignment for a class, you are intimately aware of the traditional learning environment. While our grade schools, high schools, colleges, universities, and technical schools are filled with students, most learning takes place outside these environments. That vast population of adults who are busy at some form of work composes the largest classroom. This chapter is devoted to an analysis of this population.

Of all of the issues addressed by training and development specialists, none has received the amount of attention that has been devoted to the adult learner. There is even a term to describe the process: *andragogy* (Knowles, 1984). We do not believe that such a term is necessary to understand or work with people outside the traditional classroom. It is important that you are familiar with the word, in case you want to do further reading on the subject.

Most approaches to training and development compare andragogy to pedagogy by pointing out that we should not try to teach adults the same way that we teach high school and college students. While we agree in principle, we would rather focus on the learning process of the adult and how one can be an effective trainer, rather than discussing why the pedagogical approach doesn't work with the adult. If a 23-year-old, first-line supervisor is taking a training program, we would not suggest that person be given training differently because it is at a training site rather than part of course work for a college degree in communication. We would hope that the college classroom would reflect the principles that we will elaborate in this chapter. In fact, we could argue that education nationally could benefit from the newer approaches that are used in the training field.

Without getting on a soapbox, we would suggest that most college classroom teaching would benefit from the learning approach that we will present in this chapter. Students and/or adults learn more if they are given the opportunity to integrate new information into their frames of reference. Each of us needs the opportunity to see how new information and ideas can be used. We will elaborate on this process more in the coming pages.

Who Is the Adult Learner?

Just as Shakespeare said all the world's a stage and we are merely players on it, so are we all potential adult learners. We learn every day on the job, whether it is how to use a computer or fill out a new form. We learn outside the job when we are shown how to change a tire or fix a broken chair. We are even adult learners when we learn by experience or the hard way. We learn when we are hired, fired, and even retired.

For our purposes, we need to narrow the range of adult learners and focus on those who we as trainers guide. We are interested in those who take on-the-job training, corporate classes, or any of the myriad of seminars and workshops that are offered to the public. While this does not narrow the number of potential learners, it does exclude the one-on-one training we might give or receive in the home when we learn how to make a cake or cut a piece of lumber on a straight line. We will not focus on this type of training, which we have labeled *coaching*, but the principles of working with the adult learner would certainly apply to one-on-one coaching.

Our trainee is the person who starts a new job but needs a course on how to function effectively on the job. This training could take place in a training room with a number of other trainees who need the same skills, or it could occur as individualized instruction with a videotape and a workbook. For example, telephone operators are trained in a mock switchboard room with ten to fifteen other trainees and a trainer. We are familiar with another program in which a potential backhoe operator receives training via a computer terminal and a videotape (we will elaborate on computer use in chapter 8). Once the "classroom" instruction is complete, the operator practices the skills on an actual backhoe. This type of training has long been used in the military, particularly in pilot training. In all cases, our trainees learn skills that will help them on the job.

The adult learner is also the person who receives training to upgrade or learn new skills. The authors developed typing skills long ago in high school classes but later learned that we needed to know how to use a computer for word processing. We took seminars and individualized self-help programs in the fundamentals of word processing so that we could upgrade our skills. Organizations in the public and private sectors spend billions of dollars to upgrade the skills of their employees.

Students are in school for a degree and an education. The degree usually takes a prescribed number of years, but an education takes a lifetime. As adults we are lifelong learners; it is the trainer's job to facilitate that lifelong learning process.

Key Principles of Adult Learning

We do not intend to provide a complete discussion of the learning process in this chapter. We have provided some excellent sources on learning theory in the bibliography. These sources focus on the adult in the learning process. (See, for example, the text by Knowles, 1984.) It is our intention to give you the key principles that will assist you in working effectively with adults. These principles go hand in hand with the skills necessary to be a trainer, as discussed in chapter 2.

As we said earlier in this chapter, other training books would describe adult learning as andragogy rather than pedagogy. We are convinced that all learning could benefit from the key principles that have been written about in all articles and books on adult learning. We will present these principles in order of importance.

People Learn Best by Doing

It was Confucius who said, "I hear and I forget; I see and I remember; I do and I understand." Our parents told us how to ride a bicycle, but we didn't learn until we got on and got a shove. When we learned to drive a car, reading about driving and listening to a driver's education instructor helped some, but we needed to get behind the wheel in order really to understand how to drive. We may have memorized the position of the keys on the computer keyboard, but we needed to sit in front of an actual computer before we could master the skills necessary to do word processing.

Notice the key word in the first principle: best. We are not discounting the importance of reading, hearing, seeing, and a combination of these. We are saying that we can be more effective as trainers if we follow-up by doing. A study conducted by the U.S. Department of Health, Education, and Welfare reported the following:

Learners retain:

   10 percent of what they read
   20 percent of what they hear
   30 percent of what they see
   50 percent of what they see and hear
   70 percent of what they say
   90 percent of what they say and do

There is also a corollary which says that to truly retain something we have learned, we should try to teach it to others. To teach helps you learn the material or skill better. We don't retain everything we do, but 90 percent is not bad. While the figures look suspicious in their neat ascension to 90 percent, the relationships are the important consideration. Our trainees will retain more if they can hear it as well as just read it. They will retain more if we ask them to tell us what they heard or read than if we don't.

We could put this principle another way by saying that trainees learn best by participation. Not every training program we conduct will allow trainees the opportunity actually to do what we may be presenting. For example, we may give a three-hour program on listening effectively to twenty managers. Even listening research tells us that our trainees would retain only 25 percent of what we told them after ten days. Three hours would not allow for all trainees to do all the things we might feel are necessary in order for them to develop their listening skills. We could get all of them to participate in one or two listening activities that would help them retain more than the lecture alone. Trainees need to participate in the learning process if they are going to get anything out of our programs.

We will talk more in the chapter on designing training programs about what can be accomplished in specified periods of time. Our bottom-line principle is that you should have trainees *doing* whenever possible, rather than just listening or watching. They will retain more and will consider the training more valuable.

Trainees Have Prior Experience

Trainers sometimes forget that trainees had a life before they participated in our training programs. In the next chapter we will stress the importance of doing a needs assessment before providing any training. We need to know what experiences the trainees have had on the job so we can incorporate those experiences into the training program. A trainee does not attend a training session with a clean slate, waiting for us to provide the knowledge and skills to accomplish a particular task. If our goal is to develop participative managerial skills for our trainees, we should know something about the managerial styles to which they have been exposed. Autocratic managers will react differently to our training than laissez-faire managers; in fact, both types may be very hostile to our training ideas.

The more we incorporate the life experiences of trainees into the training program, the more we can expect them to retain and use the information provided. If you recall our definition of communication, we are placing the training program within the trainees' field of experience. We will be more effective as trainers, and trainees will gain more from our program. As a trainer, you should have some knowledge of the trainees' backgrounds. If you are going to work with fire department personnel, you might want to spend some time at the fire station to see what they do.

If we combine the first two principles, we will have our trainees participating and sharing their life experiences, which will facilitate their learning and the learning of the other participants. Suppose we had Sam and Jane, two managers from a high-tech firm, in a training session on employee participation. If Sam had already attempted more employee participation, an example from him would be more effective for Jane than an example from us. As a trainer, you must both recognize and use the experience of your learners.

Effective training, like effective communication, must rely on the prior experiences of those involved in the process. Use this valuable resource rather than deny it. Failure to take advantage of the resource may be met with polite acceptance or overt hostility by the trainees. Comments like "That's interesting; we have heard it before," or "So what else is new" made to the unsuspecting trainer may lead to a false sense of security that the training program is OK, when the participants actually are saying the opposite.

Adults Have Clear Motives for Learning

"What's in it for me," or "There might be something of value that I can use," reflect the bottom-line motives of adults and all people, for that matter. If we perceive it to be in our self-interest, then we will listen and pay attention. If it is not, we won't.

As adults, we do not need instant gratification. Many of us are motivated by training that may provide a future reward rather than an immediate satisfaction. Because we have a history of past experience, we are more aware of long-term as well as short-term goals. Training can speak to those long-term and short-term goals. A colleague of ours worked with a professional football team and found out that the defense was motivated by the here-and-now while the offense could think long term. As a result, she geared the training differently for the offense and defense. We can recognize that training designed to improve our communication with supervisors may take weeks of practice before we are successful. Adults know when a trainer is offering "the pie in the sky, when we die" motivator, which is not very effective.

The problem for the trainer is that each person can and may have a different motivator. In any training session there may be as many different motivators as there are trainees. The effective trainer determines what the motivators are and incorporates them into the training program as much as possible. You seek to find what motivates the majority of trainees and incorporate that into the training.

What are some of the more common motivators that influence our behavior and acceptance of training? They include:

Monetary and nonmonetary rewards
Security
Power
Prestige
Happiness
Harmony
Meet organizational requirements
Meet organizational goals
Make work easier

A person who attends the training session because a certificate that is suitable for framing is offered may be looking for prestige. Training designed to upgrade outdated skills may motivate the person who is looking for greater security. Training designed to promote personal power may not motivate the individual who seeks greater harmony. Training that offers a fancy certificate does little for the participant seeking monetary rewards.

To avoid misinterpretation, we need to be prepared to show the participant in the last example how that certificate might lead to greater monetary rewards. We would have to indicate that the certificate demonstrates credibility, which leads to other rewards. In other words, we would relate motivators to each other to make the training more effective.

In addition to needs assessment, we can take another step to ensure that we are appealing to the primary motivators of the trainees. We ask each of our trainees to describe one thing that he or she would like to get out of the specific session. We list these on a chalkboard or flip chart and make sure that we cover them at some point during the training program. Making such a list forces us to be flexible in the topics that we cover. It could prove embarrassing if we were unable to cover each of the items listed.

Failing to motivate the trainees could cost the trainer an effective session. If trainees are not motivated enough to pay attention, they won't be interested enough to participate.

Adults Have Preoccupations

Have you ever heard someone say "I am sorry, I didn't hear you. I have a thousand things on my mind right now"? We are all pre-occupied with relationships, financial worries, deadlines, and job pressures that keep us from devoting 100 percent of our attention to something, regardless of how hard we try. Attending a training program is no different from the other competing forces; it taxes the attention spans of participants. In fact, attending a training program may heighten the preoccupations because trainees are not able to do the things they would do if they were not at the training program. We have taken them away from their work or, even worse, we may have asked them to give up leisure time to attend a training session.

We have at least two alternatives for dealing with the pre-occupations. We can approach directly what may be bothering the participants if they all seem to be preoccupied with the same issues. In one workshop, the participants, city police officers, were upset with the previous trainer because he called them names and generally viewed them as second-class citizens. While that trainer may have had a valid purpose, any trainer who followed such a session had a preoccupied group. The officers' hostility had to be dealt with before any additional training could be covered. It was, and the session continued with only the first half hour lost to the preoccupation. Actually, it made the second trainer's task easier because of the willingness to consider the needs of the officers.

Second, we can lessen the impact of preoccupations by making sure that we are constantly involving the trainees and addressing their needs. Like reading a good book, time will pass quickly and the participants will be so involved that they will not think of those preoccupations. Variety in both content and delivery can lessen the impact of distractions.

As a corollary to this principle, homework should be kept to a minimum. Since trainees have so many demands on their time, they cannot be expected to spend a lot of time working outside the training sessions. Of course, if we have designed an effective program, our participants will want to integrate the new informa-tion or skills into their daily lives, so it will not be perceived as homework, but as practice. If our trainees are motivated, we can ask more of them than we can of those who are at a training session because they were told to be there.

Any homework should focus on the practice of some skill rather than on reading a certain amount of material. This varies with the type of trainees and the goals for the training program. You might want top executive trainees to read a current book on management practices, but you would not require potential backhoe operators to read the operations manual for the equipment. Both types should be made aware of whatever reading materials are available for reference.

These are the four key principles that need to be considered by the trainer, regardless of the training environment. Adult learners are pragmatic individuals, preoccupied with many demands on their time, motivated by self-interest, and attentive to those things that they can learn by doing. When we offer training, we need to keep these issues uppermost in our minds. We are now even suggesting that supplemental materials be available in the back of the training room should the trainees want them. If we have successfully motivated them in the training session, they will want to read more.

Secondary Learning Issues

As if these four principles were not enough, there are a number of other issues that we need to be aware of as we work with adults. These issues apply differently to adult learners; what might be a barrier to one could be a challenge to another. We will look at five such issues.

Coping with Change

One objective of every class we teach is important to training: the ability to cope with change. Many trainees will look upon change as a threat to existing values and habits. New ideas in a training program can be seen as a threat to job security, as the first step in being replaced, or as a change that will make performance of a job more difficult. We must integrate change into the training program so that it is a challenge rather than a threat. If we tie change to the four learning principles discussed earlier, we can be successful. For example, we could demonstrate to middle-management trainees how employee participation could reduce conflict and increase productivity without reducing management's ability to manage. Failing to make this connection will result in a resistance to all training and our trainees will go away unhappy and maybe even angry.

Just as some trainees fear change, others look forward to the challenge as a way to relieve the boredom of a given task. Our job is much easier when we work with this group of learners, and working with this eager group can be a very positive experience.

Avoiding Jargon

As we discussed earlier, adult learners have a broad range of experiences and as a result do not like to be talked down to. Colleagues may be impressed because we can use terms like "ethos," "pathos," and "logos," but trainees will demand that we "cut the bull." Using jargon is an excellent example of talking down to a group of trainees. If our suggestions in chapter 2 are followed on how to be a credible trainer, jargon won't be necessary to establish high credibility, but it can sure lessen one's credibility and kill learning.

Every learning situation requires that the trainer walk a fine line between providing needed information and skipping the basics. We could say "push the envelope" (jargon), or we could say "keep finding new ways that are more productive." We are letting the sophisticated trainee know we are aware of current thinking and not using the jargon terms. Chapter 4 on conducting a needs assessment will offer some concrete suggestions. The better we know our trainee audience, the clearer the fine line will be.

Handling Immediate Feedback

When a trainee suggests that a particular example provided by the trainer is wrong, we are given immediate feedback to our training. Adult learners are more than willing to let us know what they think about our ideas, concepts, and training activities. If they like what we are doing or saying, we will know it; likewise, we clearly know when we are off the mark. College students may sit in class and write letters, daydream, or look interested when they are not. Trainees are more likely to start talking to each other, ask you questions, or just tell you that they don't agree with what you are saying.

Unlike other learning issues, immediate feedback has a great impact on the trainer. What do you say when a participant says you don't know what you are talking about? While we might want to tell that participant a thing or two, we would have to react in a way to facilitate the training program. We could ask that person to elaborate so that we could determine where we might differ. If we are well prepared and have conducted a thorough needs assessment, this won't happen often.

Accommodating Different Learning Styles

Adults, like all learners, learn at different rates and in different ways. Some people have the ability to learn material in a short period of time, while it may take others three and four times as long. Within limits, we can design a training program to fit the learning rates for the majority of trainees. If we are fortunate, we can offer a training module that allows participants to proceed at their own rates. Individualized instruction solves the problem of learner rate, but increases the cost in time and money to the organization providing the training.

Cognitive Mapping

Cognitive mapping is a psychological educational term that describes how a person learns best. As we said earlier in the chapter, we retain only so much information by reading, seeing, and hearing. Individuals differ in which senses help them learn best. Some people learn best by reading at their own pace; others learn best by listening to a speaker or a tape. While we cannot offer five or six variations of a training program geared to five or six different groups of learners, we can offer that variety within one training program. We should incorporate all of the senses in the learning process. That is why we offer entire chapters of this text on the computer as well as audiovisual material.

Providing Real-World Focus

Finally, adult learners prefer training that is problem-centered and real-world focused, rather than theoretical and abstract. If we are working with employees of the ABC Corporation, we should not use case studies from XYZ Corporation if we can get participants' examples from ABC. We can incorporate theoretical material into training in a practical way. We have other ways of describing the Theory X versus Theory Y approaches; we could even ask the participants to describe the ABC Corporation in terms of Theory X and Theory Y without applying these labels until we summarize the concepts.

Whether your trainees are over 30 or under 20, comfortable seating and regular breaks are necessary. Such considerations should be second nature to the training environment. We do not dismiss these issues of adult learning, but feel the need to focus on just the key principles.

We have deliberately addressed those principles of adult learning that may be missed by the trainer who comes from an educational background as a student or teacher. Essentially, we are presenting sound educational principles that are applicable whether you are teaching or training adults or the young.

Summary

A good trainer is user oriented just as a good communicator is receiver oriented. At all times in the training session, we are concerned with what our adult learner is getting from the program. Are we facilitating the learning process or just presenting material?

For adult learners, we will focus on *doing* rather than just listening or watching. We will use their experiences and motivators to help them get the most from the training. We will place the training program in a proper perspective, recognizing that training is only a part of their lives. We will be practical and concrete in approach, and adapt not only to the trainees' needs, but also to their learning rates and styles.

Since training is a process like communication, we can constantly adapt and modify our training to meet the changing demands of the trainees. We can repeat points and provide different examples when needed. This can only happen, however, if we are trainee or user oriented.

Doing a Needs Assessment

Objectives

This chapter will help you

▶ understand the purposes of a needs assessment

▶ recognize the components of a needs assessment

▶ identify the procedures involved in a needs assessment

▶ recognize the nature of the audience of a needs assessment

Introduction

The first step in effective training and development is to find out what the organization and employees need. As earlier chapters have pointed out, the nature of these needs is not self-evident. This chapter presents various ways of conducting a needs assessment, which is the process of identifying issues to be addressed in an organization.

Purposes of Needs Assessment

If employees knew exactly what they needed to learn, they could request certain kinds of training, learn those skills, apply the knowledge on the job, and then work "happily ever after." If managers could identify accurately their own and their employees' learning needs, they too would work in an ideal environment. The reality, however, is that problems at work are expressed indirectly. Poor performance, low morale, and a host of other job-related problems are symptoms, and they cannot be taken only at face value. Individuals and teams may know that something is wrong, but usually are not able to identify exactly what that is.

There are many reasons why employees and managers have trouble identifying the real nature of problems. One is that they are, in a sense, too close to the problem. They know what is wrong in terms of how it affects them, but they do not see the problem in relation to the whole company. Take, for example, Jake, whose job is to deal with customers over the phone. Suppose Jake begins to hear nothing but complaints from customers who call in. From his perspective, Jake may conclude, "The customers sure are grumpy these days. They all need lessons in courtesy." He logically may blame several things for the complaints: customers are dissatisfied with the product; the weather has adverse effects on people's moods; or there's too much bad news in the media. Because his perspective is limited to the scope of his job, Jake is likely to be unaware of company-related circumstances that might cause customer dissatisfaction—for example, a recent decision by the accounting department to pressure customers to pay more quickly, or a new marketing program that makes promises beyond the true capacities of the product. The point is that because Jake's view is not broad enough, he is unaware of other organizational circumstances that affect customers and therefore have a direct impact on his job.

Another reason it is hard to identify the real problem is that so many possible interpretations exist. Everyone has his or her own ideas about why things go well, or do not go well, and what should be done about it. At work, every person's performance affects everyone else's, no matter how indirectly. To really address the issue, an organization must synthesize various points of view to get a more complete picture of the problem.

A needs analysis is the process of getting as many views as feasible within the constraints of time, money, and the scope of the problem. The first purpose of the needs assessment, then, is to gather relevant data to help define the problem. When the views are collected, through the various means discussed in this chapter, the organization has a clearer picture of what is going on. In this sense, the needs assessment is a diagnosis of the organization's health.

A second purpose of the needs analysis is to provide a background for alternative solutions to the problem. In the process of collecting data—that is, information about symptoms of the problem—the trainer can get a sense of what solutions individual managers and employees think would be appropriate. For example, Jake, dealing with customers over the phone, may think that the "real" problem is marketing's unrealistic promises, and that the solution is to have marketing stop their overreaching campaign. Tracey, who works in marketing, may think the "real" problem is that employees in customer service are rude to customers, and that the solution is to train the employees to explain, in more detail and with more enthusiasm, the features of the product. Brooke, in accounting, may think the "real" problem is the outdated billing system, and the solution is to buy a new billing program. By synthesizing these— and other—views, the trainer gains an idea of the kinds of solutions that might work.

A third purpose of the needs analysis is to create within the organization an atmosphere of support for training programs the company ultimately will provide. If the firm were simply to tell employees "This is what's wrong, and this is how we are going to fix it," strong resistance would be a natural reaction. Even if top management were right, employees would resent its top-down approach. Although this always has been true, it is even more apparent today, as employer organizations become increasingly more team oriented and less hierarchical. By conducting a needs analysis, which asks for input from individuals at all levels of the organization, the firm is telling all employees and managers—all members of the team—that their input matters. The inclusive, participative nature of the needs assessment tends to reduce the likelihood of resistance and increase the likelihood of support. If support exists throughout the organization, solutions such as training programs are more likely to be well received—and effective.

Components of the Needs Assessment

While every needs assessment has unique features to match those of the organization, eight issues to consider are common in all needs assessments.

Timing

The first component is the timing of the needs assessment. If employees are under pressure, for example, they may be too hurried or distracted to give full attention to questions being asked of them. Or, if top management has just announced a new policy—say, longer or shorter vacations—the employees' comments may relate more to the immediate event than to an overall picture of the work environment. Suppose you were asked to do a needs assessment immediately following the announced layoff of a thousand employees. How might other employees view the timing of your task? They may think you are "spying" or helping management decide who gets laid off. To get accurate information, the needs analysis must take place under conditions that are as close to "normal" as possible. However, continual change, downsizing, fear of layoffs, high stress and other negative factors are part of the "normal" environment in many workplaces today. Trainers, therefore, must distinguish between *incident*-related stress and the "normal" high-stress atmosphere.

Participation

The second component is participation. Should everyone in the organization be involved in the needs analysis? While this may be ideal, it is extremely costly in terms of both time and money. It also is not necessary, because random selection of employees probably provides views that represent the entire organization. Sometimes, only certain departments need to be involved. To be effective, a needs analysis must get information from the appropriate sources. In a construction company, for example, the owner was concerned about delays on one project. He checked with his foremen, they checked with their crews, yet no cause for the delays could be identified. After much wasted time and through a casual remark to his secretary, the owner learned the delay was caused by problems involving paperwork in the office. By focusing only on the field crews, the owner had overlooked important sources of information. It is important to identify all relevant departments, and to include appropriate and/or representative employees from those departments.

Confidentiality

A third component is the confidentiality of information that is gathered. Most commonly, needs analyses focus on the issues raised, and not on who raised which issues. The confidentiality of the sources of information allows individuals to speak more freely. It also helps them believe that management is trying to focus on issues rather than spying on them. Trainers' reputations follow them. This is true for both external consultants and internal trainers. Confidentiality may be harder for internal trainers to maintain, because they work daily with the same people, develop friendships, and prefer certain individuals over others. Those who maintain confidentiality will find it easier to work with the same employees "next time," and those who don't, won't.

Selection of Issues

A fourth consideration is how to select the issues to be examined. For example, the company may preselect certain issues that will come under scrutiny; e.g., management may want to examine leadership, job satisfaction, or compensation. Once the issues are chosen, the needs analysis will be aimed at learning about them. The opposite, or emergent, approach is to use general, open-ended questions, such as "How are things going in the company (or agency)?," to find out what issues emerge as important to employees.

Whether a needs analysis takes the preselected approach or the emergent approach depends on the organization's intentions. The *preselected approach* provides answers to what top management wants to know; the *emergent approach* seeks to find out what employees think is important. Both approaches have advantages and disadvantages.

In the preselected approach, one advantage is that management is able to focus on what it wants to find out. Another advantage is that employees simply answer what is asked, without having to think of issues themselves; this may save time and money. A third advantage is that employees learn which issues are important to management. This approach also has disadvantages, however. First, employees may resent the fact that they have no input about which issues are important to the company, in which case management would be making things worse by asking any questions at all. Second, management's questions may focus more on the symptoms than on the real problems, and the view may be too narrow to identify real issues. Third, because of either the resentment employees feel or the symptomatic nature of the issues, management may get distorted responses.

The emergent approach has the advantage of allowing employees to speak their minds and identify any issues they consider significant, thereby helping them feel included and important. A second advantage is that the issues identified are likely to be close to the real problems, at least from the employees' points of view. A third advantage is that because they had input, employees are more likely to support programs based on emergent issues. A disadvantage to this method is that it is time-consuming to unearth issues from answers to open-ended questions. The answers are likely to be broad and long, requiring time to sort through. A second disadvantage is that because of the time involved, this method is costly. A third is the risk that employees may expect all the issues they've identified to be addressed. Because not all issues can be addressed—at least, not at one time—care must be taken to alert employees to this fact. Otherwise, their expectations will be unrealistically high and they will perceive any solutions as falling short.

Company Philosophy

The fifth component of a needs assessment is the degree to which the needs analysis is part of company philosophy. If a firm's general management philosophy is to tell rather than ask, a needs assessment may cause resentment or, even worse, suspicion on the part of employees. If, however, the company continually asks for input from all levels, the needs assessment will be perceived as a natural or appropriate event. This is especially true today, as both companies and government agencies move more towards participative, and even decision-making, teamwork.

Target Population

The sixth issue is the target population—those individuals, departments, levels, or other categories that are going to be included in the questioning process. The size of the group may affect the number or types of questions that can be asked.

For example, if you were doing a needs analysis in a restaurant that had ten employees, the group is small enough for you to include everyone. In a larger restaurant chain employing five hundred people, however, you probably would make random selections of representatives from each job type.

The area of specialization of a department may influence the kind of information that can be gathered. If you were interviewing engineers, for example, you could expect them to talk about the technical side of their work. When you interviewed the sales staff, however, you would be more likely to hear about personalities and stress.

Employees' levels of sophistication also can affect the type of information you get. For example, experienced, computer-literate employees are likely to describe symptoms that relate to the *system*; employees who are unfamiliar with, or resistant to, computers are likely to describe symptoms that relate to *their* terminal, boss, customer, or department.

Specific Method

The seventh component is the specific method used to do a needs assessment. A variety of methods is presented in the next section. The important consideration, however, is that each method has its own impact on different groups. Methods must be chosen on the basis of what will be most effective for each group. For example, interviews might be appropriate for small groups, while questionnaires would be better for large ones.

Depth

The eighth component is the depth of the needs analysis, or how much personal and emotional commitment it draws from employees. The appropriate depth varies with each situation, but a general rule is to go "only as deep as you have to." It is both ineffective and unprofessional to become more involved than necessary. As an example, one consultant we know did a needs assessment for a bottling firm. Instead of limiting his questions to the immediate issues—such as employees' opinions about company morale and opportunities for advancement—he began asking whether any employees drank alcohol on the job. Because his questions were deeper than the situation called for, he created distrust, suspicion and fear among the employees and was unable to finish his project.

These eight components give the trainer ways to identify appropriate methods for a needs assessment. The trainer is then ready to select a needs assessment procedure.

Procedure for Needs Assessments

The number of ways in which to conduct a needs assessment probably matches the number of individuals doing them. Key ways to do a needs assessment include interviews, questionnaires, sensing, polling, confrontation meetings, and observation.

Interviews

Our professional preference is to use the interview as the first step in the assessment process whenever possible. We would recommend that you interview everyone you can, from the top person down through the organization. This may not always be possible if you were invited into the company by a manager to look at a specific department. But try to get a total picture of the organization you are assessing.

Who and how many people should you interview? We make it a point to interview people at each level and division in the organization. If the organization is small (for example, fewer than fifty employees), we may be able to interview everyone. If there are more than fifty employees, we can select employees in such a way as to give us a good cross section of the company. Your contact person can provide you with an organizational chart that should assist you in selecting interviewees.

The interview provides us with useful information that we can incorporate in questionnaires we might use. In one assessment, we discovered in interviews that employees apparently were not aware of career training opportunities within the company, so we developed a series of questions on career development training.

The interview method provides a personal touch, with all its benefits and limitations. Questions may be structured—that is, aimed at getting "yes-no" or other specific answers—or unstructured—that is, open-ended enough to require employees to raise issues of concern to them. The following structured questions were part of an interview with engineers:

1. For what kinds of jobs do you write proposals?
2. What is the average length of your reports?
3. Do your reports follow a prescribed format, or do you choose your own?

The following *un*structured questions were used in the interview with the engineers' clients:

1. How effective are the proposals the engineers write?
2. In what areas do you think the engineers might need help?
3. How creative are the engineers' proposals?

You can see that the interviewer will get a vivid picture by varying the types of questions used and comparing the answers from each point of view. Through this process, a sensitive interviewer can glean a great deal of information from nuances, nonverbal behavior, and a host of other communication patterns, in addition to the answers themselves.

The interview establishes a great deal of rapport between employees and the interviewer. This rapport can contribute to support for the needs assessment itself and for the new programs it brings about. A limitation of interviews, however, is that more personal and emotional information than is useful may emerge. For example, during interviews one of the authors conducted in a hospital, many employees vented frustrations about their spouses. While this problem was real to the employees, it related only indirectly to the organizational issues. It also was the kind of problem that should be addressed in personal counseling, rather than in organizational training.

The interview method requires a great deal of time. Another negative aspect is that the interviewer's skills greatly influence the richness of the data collected. If more than one person does the interviews, responses may not be equivalent.

Questionnaires and Instruments

A questionnaire is the traditional method by which employees respond anonymously to a series of questions. While the questions could come after an emergent approach is used—that is, a questionnaire based on earlier input from employees—most deal with issues that are preselected.

There are a variety of issues that you can address through questionnaire assessments. The primary purpose for questionnaires is to provide the trainer with employee perceptions of some aspect of the organization. Exhibit 4.1 contains a very generic questionnaire about nurses' perceptions of their roles in a hospital environment. The questions cover topics from work load to credibility; none goes into depth on the issues. On the positive side, the questionnaire is brief and assures the nurses of anonymity.

Exhibit 4.1   Nurses' Perceptions

Please circle the number that represents your opinion about each statement.

	Strongly Agree				Strongly Disagree	
1. Nurses' skills are well respected by physicians in this hospital.	1	2	3	4	5	6
2. Nurses have too little to say about how their departments are run.	1	2	3	4	5	6
3. I am pleased with my work hours.	1	2	3	4	5	6
4. The nurse's role includes making decisions about treatments for patients.	1	2	3	4	5	6
5. The hospital administration shows a great deal of support for nurses.	1	2	3	4	5	6

At the other end of the continuum, some organizations ask employees to complete a ten- to fifteen-page survey on a regular basis. These surveys cover all aspects of the organization, from working conditions to career development. The success of lengthy questionnaires depends on management support and enthusiasm. If employees are asked every year for their opinions but the results are neither shared nor acted upon, employee cooperation will wane. In a survey for a high-tech firm, we distributed more than five hundred questionnaires to the hourly employees and received twenty completed ones. The time the company wanted the surveys distributed coincided with media reports of the plant's closing and a major holiday season. You can see several of our eight guidelines were violated in this assessment by the person who requested the analysis.

Questionnaires also can be designed to focus on specific issues within the organization. If interview information suggests that a specific topic is important, a questionnaire can be used to determine how widespread the concern is. Interviews in one local government agency led us to conclude that teamwork and cooperation were lacking. We asked the employees to respond to a series of questions concerning leadership, teamwork, and cooperation. We combined the interview data with the survey results and presented a series of recommendations for training in that area.

Four other factors should be considered as you develop questionnaires. First, you do not have to develop every survey from scratch. There are a number of questionnaires that have been used by both trainers and researchers that could aid you in designing questions. The bibliography at the end of this book provides numerous examples of questionnaires, whose topics range from organizational culture to communication satisfaction. You may want to use preexisting questionnaires, so be sure they meet your needs and that you have made appropriate arrangements with the survey developer (who owns the copyright). It may be easy to use a generic questionnaire, but you must make sure it fits the organization you are assessing.

Most questionnaires are in the form of statements with which a respondent can agree or disagree. The sample questionnaire in Exhibit 4.1 is in this form, which we call *Likert scales*. Choices for responding to these statements allow for degrees of feeling, ranging from strongly agreeing to strongly disagreeing and including several choices in between. Other choices might range from very frequently to never. We recommend this format because it is easy for the respondent to understand and complete. We also recommend that you read one of the research methods texts for a more complete discussion of survey development (see Babbie, 1985).

Another issue is who and how many people should get your survey. Ideally it would be desirable to survey everyone in the organization, but this is not always practical. Survey everyone in organizations with fewer than fifty employees. With larger organizations, make certain you survey employees at each level and within each division. You must make certain that you don't survey just one person at a level or department, for the results could be biased and the anonymity of the respondent would be lost. Beyond these guidelines, we try to get our questionnaires into the hands of as many employees as we can.

When you consider a questionnaire, be sure you plan for each audience. For example, if you are assessing a supermarket chain, you will want to get feedback from customers as well as from employees. In today's customer-oriented company and government agency, clients and customers—*external and internal*—should be included, along with department employees, as respondents. When a department in one firm wanted to know how effectively it communicated, we surveyed all employees in the department, all the department's clients within the firm, and all its external customers. Each departmental employee got feedback about how his or her communication was perceived by departmental coworkers, organizational clients, and external customers.

A final concern in the development of a survey is the use of open-ended questions. As in interviews, open-ended questions allow the respondent some freedom in giving you useful information. You might ask employees to describe what they like best about their jobs and what they like least. While open-ended questions are not easily coded for computer analysis, the information can be invaluable. In an assessment completed by our students, they found agreement between the interview data and the open-ended responses but nothing useful in the Likert-type items. Analysis of the Likert-type items indicated they were too generic and, in some cases, internally inconsistent. The assessment was not lost, however, because the students used several sources of information.

Questionnaires are relatively inexpensive and therefore make it easier to get information from everyone in the company. They simplify the confidentiality of responses and provide anonymity, which probably increases the likelihood of honest answers. Questionnaires also lend themselves to statistical processing. On the negative side, questionnaires lack the personal touch and too often do not allow for employee input in terms of content.

Sensing

This method is the same as the interview method, except that a select number of employees participate. The interviewees may be employees who are dissatisfied with something, a group on whom a pilot program has been tested, or individuals with some other characteristic that distinguishes them from the rest of the firm. One positive outcome of this method is that management is exposed to diverse views. Another is that programs may be designed for specific groups. One limitation is that this method may be perceived by employees as spying. Another limitation is that the effectiveness of the method depends on both the groups' willingness to be honest and the interviewer's skills.

Polling

Through this method, a group surveys its members to find out how people feel or think about current issues: Do we have too many meetings? How much influence on the company do I feel I have? How quickly and how well does management share its decisions? As an example, your boss might chat with each employee one day, asking, "How do you feel about the parking arrangements?" or "What would you think of us holding weekly staff meetings?"

This method works best in groups of five to thirty. The benefits are that polling is fast and includes the entire group. A limitation is that the questions are not designed professionally and may not be useful outside of a specific group.

Confrontation Meetings

The confrontation is one in which individuals involved in a problem meet to discuss the problem openly. Generally, this kind of meeting cannot take place as a first step; rather, it follows preliminary work that includes individual interviews with the participants. The individual talks help create trust and support, both of which are required for effective confrontation meetings. A benefit of this method is that it is participative and gives everyone a chance to raise issues, learn others' views, and share ideas. A limitation is that a great deal of skill is required on the part of the facilitator to neutralize potentially explosive situations and to create an atmosphere in which people will communicate openly and calmly.

Observation

Management by Walking Around (Peters & Waterman, 1982) is a fine way to do a needs assessment. If a manager's regular behavior includes talking and visiting with employees, the manager gets a first-hand view of how things are going. By doing this regularly, the manager gains trust from the employees and is less likely to be seen as spying than is a manager who only shows up occasionally to ask questions.

These general procedures comprise needs assessment methods. It is important to remember that each organization is unique, and that every method must be adapted to fit the situation.

Audience for Needs Assessments

Even before needs assessment begins, the trainer must recognize who the audience is going to be. Everyone within an organization is a potential member of the audience. Depending on the situation, an individual may have a number of different roles: part of the target population during the needs assessment, a member of the audience when the assessment is complete, and a participant in training programs that follow the assessment.

Top Management

Top management is an audience that wants to know the needs to be addressed for greater company effectiveness. Top management's concerns involve the long-term success of the firm; if employees' needs go unmet, the results are poor performance, low-quality work output, and dissatisfied customers or clients. If needs are met, the results are often good performance, quality work, and satisfied customers or clients. Because top management's planning affects the future of the company, the managers must know what needs exist and then plan ways to meet these needs.

Top management has its own views and goals, and these must be included in the needs assessment. For example, suppose top management believes in promoting new managers from within, instead of hiring them from outside. One focus of any needs assessment within such a company would include ways of identifying the needs of employees who have the potential for, and interest in, becoming managers.

Managers

Individual managers within the organization comprise another part of the audience. These managers are responsible for the immediate performance of their employees, so they, too, want to know what needs must be met. In addition, managers have their own ideas about what needs exist for themselves and for their employees, so their views must be considered.

As an example, the manager of a fast-food restaurant has many part-time employees whose jobs involve dealing with the public. The manager probably would want the needs assessment to include ways of finding out the strengths and weaknesses of his or her employees' consumer-relations skills. At the same time, the manager would make sure the trainer conducted the needs assessment at various times of day, so all appropriate part-time help could be included.

Team Leaders

Team leaders make up another segment of the audience. Their roles are ambiguous—they guide and represent their work teams, but they do not have the authority of supervisors or managers. Team leaders rely on participation, cooperation, feedback, cross-training, and numerous other methods of continually improving team performance. They want input from internal customers (such as managers, other departments, and other teams), external customers (the final users of their products or services), and each other.

As an example, computer services installs computers for the firm's sales department. The sales department is an internal client of computer services. Customers who buy products through the sales department are external customers—not only of the sales department, but also of computer services. If the sales department's computers are reliable, the external customers benefit because they can order any time they want to; if the sales department's computers are down a lot, the external customer is inconvenienced. In this situation, the team leader within computer services is likely to want the needs assessment to include input from external customers as well as from the sales department.

Employees

Employees at all levels are an audience. They know the details of their work and many of the company programs are aimed at them. The accuracy of their input is crucial to the success of the needs assessment, as is their acceptance of the results.

Suppose, for example, the desk clerks in a hotel are told to take a course in first aid. Their first reaction may be "Why?" because they do not see an immediate need. Even if they finally agree, they may resist management's method of forcing this course on them. In this example, the main problem is that the employees know nothing about needs identified through an assessment process. Instead, they are simply told to take a course. Had the trainer recognized them as an audience, however, the clerks would have been included at the start of the needs assessment, and through their involvement in the data-gathering process, the clerks would have become aware of, and more receptive to, identified needs. When employees are included from the beginning of the process, they are more open to the results.

Trainers

The trainer is a special audience for the needs assessment. It is the trainer's role to design the assessment in ways that produce legitimate identification of needs. The trainer's role also means using this information effectively: designing programs that meet identified needs.

Knowing that he or she will design programs on the basis of the needs assessment, the trainer must make sure the assessment provides information both of the right type and in a useful form. For example, a consultant was called in by an electronics firm to help a trainer, Steve, design a needs assessment. Steve was looking for specific information: what kind of training in communication did employees need? He had planned to ask employees directly: "How much do you know about the communication process?", "What areas of communication are you weak in?", and similar questions. This plan would have resulted in useless types of information based on individuals' self-perceptions of their communication skills, rather than uniform or shared definitions of communication. Steve also would have gotten this information in a form he could not use: personal opinions with no common scale of measurement.

The approach actually taken was to break communication into specific behavioral definitions. In this case, management turned out to be interested in public-speaking skills. Next, Steve identified ways of measuring the degree of a person's success in this skill. As criteria he used audience evaluations and top management's ratings of speakers. He then grouped speakers as excellent, average, or poor. Interviewing representatives randomly selected from each group, Steve asked questions that called for short, simple answers: "How much time do you spend rehearsing a speech?", "Do you use note cards or read from typed pages?", and so forth.

Steve got information of the right type: in this case, answers about each speaker's preparation and style. He also got the information in a useful form: answers that were either yes-no or numerical in terms of length of time. Because of their type and form, the data could now be compared and interpreted. By seeing themselves as part of the audience, trainers are better able to design needs assessments in ways that are useful to them.

Customers and Clients

Customers and clients also are audiences for needs assessments because they receive the final result of training programs: the actual products or services they get from an organization. They also are the reason for the organization's existence. In the past, customers and clients were not involved in needs assessments because they were not directly involved with the company's day-to-day activities. However, today's focus on customer orientation emphasizes the importance of including customers in needs assessments. Because they are the "ultimate decision-makers" about the value of the products, services, and the company or agency, customer/client input is extremely valuable.

When changes occur in a firm, customers and clients usually know this quickly. Whether changes are for better or worse depends, to a great extent, on training, which, in turn, depends on the accuracy and usefulness of a needs assessment. Take, for example, a drugstore where the cashiers are unfriendly. Customers may be attracted to the store because of convenience or low prices. Some potential customers may avoid the store, despite convenience or prices, because of the unfriendliness. If a needs assessment were done in this store, and *if it included customer input*, one result might be interpersonal skills training for the cashiers. If the training were effective, customers would quickly notice the change.

Changes in management, in policies, or in other areas can have a negative effect on employees who otherwise are content. These changes, too, are quickly noticed by customers. The job of the trainer is to include customers' views in the needs assessment, and to make sure the outcome will have a positive effect on them. The effect on customers determines, ultimately, the success of the firm.

Summary

Needs assessments affect everyone in the organization, and indirectly affect everyone outside of it who deals with the organization. Useful needs assessments are based on specific purposes, have key components, follow certain procedures, and are aimed at various audiences. Purposes include defining a problem, providing a background for solutions, and creating support for training programs. Key components are made up of timing, participants, confidentiality, issue selection (preselected or emergent), company philosophy, target population, specific method, and depth of analysis. Interviews, questionnaires, sensing, polls, meetings, and observation make up the methods for a needs assessment, while the audience includes managers, team leaders, employees, the trainers themselves, and customers. As a basis for training programs, needs assessments serve as a diagnosis of what an organization needs to do to improve its effectiveness.

Presenting Proposals and Assessments

Objectives

This chapter will help you

► identify the three types of proposals for training
► design proposals for effective presentations
► recognize the differences in pre-assessment and needs-assessment proposals
► understand training proposals

Introduction

If we did everything that was outlined in the previous chapter, the result is a thorough needs assessment of an organization, and we need to know just exactly what to do with it. In this chapter, we will talk about how one goes about presenting needs assessments and even proposals to do needs assessments, as well as how to present training proposals to management.

Comments that we have to make here will apply both to the in-house trainer and, even more so, to a consultant who has been retained by an organization. Needless to say, the outside consultant has a bigger job in presenting proposals and assessments because the bottom line for this consultant is his or her very livelihood. The in-house consultant may have the security of being an employee of the organization, but still needs to make a strong case for the assessment and the training. We will take a look at presenting proposals and assessments in the rest of this chapter.

Types of Proposals

Essentially, there are three types of proposals that you can make. We will discuss each type and provide examples, as well as a sample outline for how you might develop a written proposal, which then may serve as a basis for any kind of oral report you may have to or will want to make.

Needs-Assessment Proposals

The first proposal one needs to be familiar with is making a proposal to do a needs assessment. This proposal precedes any needs assessment we might do of an organization. Essentially, what we are saying to our superior, or to the chief executive officer (CEO) if we are an outside consultant, is we think there is a need to take a look at your organization. We would like to propose that an assessment of the organization be made. Sometimes we are asked to do an assessment because the CEO believes there is a need. For example, recently we made a proposal of about eight pages to an organization at their request suggesting that they hire us to do a needs assessment. After we submitted this proposal to do a needs assessment, we were told, "No, the organization will do its own needs assessment," but they wanted to hire us to do training on what was found as a result of doing the needs assessment.

What, then, goes into a proposal to conduct a needs assessment? It doesn't vary that much from the needs assessment itself, but simply is a proposal and requires more justification as to why a needs assessment ought to be done. There are three parts to the proposal, as can be seen in the outline in Exhibit 5.1. We would like to discuss each of these three components in some detail.

Exhibit 5.1　Proposal to Conduct a Needs Assessment

> Executive Summary (one page or less)
> Proposed Parameters of the Needs Assessment
> Proposed Procedures
> 　Population of the assessment
> 　Sampling plan
> 　Methodology
> 　Means of analysis

Executive summary.　The executive summary is the best shot we have to convince whoever reads the proposal that we ought to conduct it. In essence, it is a persuasive communication that encapsules the entire proposal in a page or less. Why include an executive summary? The answer is clear if one considers the amount of information that decision-makers have to read on a daily basis. If managers and CEOs are bombarded with a volume of information, they will look for ways to shortcut the process and extract only the relevant information. The executive summary provides that vehicle to aid the manager in decision making. In some cases the manager may circulate the summary to other top managers for review. They may never see or make a decision on the entire proposal.

This executive summary contains an overview, as well as key persuasive arguments to convince the person in charge that this needs assessment ought to be done. The summary must have the ability to stand alone in case it is deliberately separated from the proposal for review. Give the arguments but save the rationale and support material for the proposal.

Proposed parameters.　The second major section of this proposal discusses the parameters, as well as the need for conducting a needs assessment. For example, rumors may be running rampant within an organization and on the basis of the widespread nature of the rumors, we might propose that a needs assessment be done to ascertain not only the source of the rumors, but what might be done vis-à-vis training to reduce the rumors and the tension that may be resulting from them. This section contains a major persuasive appeal for conducting a needs assessment.

The parameters might also set out the scope of the assessment. Many times the organization may want you to focus on a particular department or cost center. We recall a student group who was asked to present a proposal to a restaurant but was told up front not to include the kitchen staff. This became a parameter for the assessment. Any limitation that is presented up front is considered a parameter which must be acknowledged.

Some parameters may make the assessment a waste of time. To complete an analysis of a restaurant without exploring the kitchen staff and its relationship to the rest of the organization would be of little value. On the other hand if you are trying to learn how to complete a needs assessment (i.e., a student), it may be a good learning experience.

By putting the parameters in the proposal, you are signalling the person for whom the assessment is to be done what limitations there might be on the final assessment. Clearly it would be that person's decision to move forward with the assessment.

We are not doing the needs assessment at this point, but simply describing in some detail the reasons the needs assessment ought to be done, as well as the scope of the proposed needs assessment. We are making the sales pitch for the assessment.

Proposed procedures. The last major section describes the procedures that we would use in order to conduct a viable needs assessment. We want to describe the total population that would be affected by the needs assessment, as well as any procedure we might use to sample from within the organization. So, if we were working in an organization of 10,000 employees, we might say that the population affected by the needs assessment would be all 10,000, but that we would want to sample half of the employees randomly, or maybe a tenth of the employees going across all of the levels within the organization. This would give us a sampling plan and statistically we could work out how representative this sample would be of the overall population.

In our proposed procedures, we would want to discuss the methods by which we would conduct our needs assessment. We described these methods in some detail in the previous chapter, so that information should be incorporated in the proposal we would present to our manager or to a CEO.

In our proposal, we would want to conclude the procedures section by describing how we would analyze the data and determine whether the results warrant further management time, and whether training might be called for.

This assessment analysis might incorporate some statistics. However, you would not want to incorporate "t-tests" or "analysis of variance" if these concepts were Greek to the person reading the report. On the other hand, if the manager or CEO has some statistical background, failure to incorporate such procedures into your proposed analysis would probably result in your not getting the go-ahead to do the needs assessment. You would not want the manager to ask you why you did not use multiple regression if you do not mention statistical procedures.

These three major components of a needs-assessment proposal would average between five and ten pages of description. It is not a good idea to spell out in too much detail what would be done. Otherwise, if you were an outside consultant, the organization could use your proposal and not bother hiring you to do the actual assessment. Your task, then, is to entice the manager into the need for a needs assessment without revealing too much information.

We are making the assumption here that a proposal is necessary before conducting a needs assessment. Sometimes organizations simply assume that needs assessments will be conducted on a periodic basis, and thus no such proposals would be necessary. These organizations view the annual assessment of employee attitudes as an integral part of their commitment to effective management.

Needs Assessment

Assuming we have the go-ahead to do a needs assessment, what, then, should be incorporated in the actual assessment? Exhibit 5.2 contains an outline for the typical assessment, whether it's being done in-house or by an outside consultant.

Again, you can see that the executive summary is a critical portion of the assessment. Unlike the proposal that we described earlier, in the actual needs assessment you will incorporate the results of the executive summary. No longer are we proposing; we are now describing what we found and the means by which we found it.

Exhibit 5.2 Needs-Assessment Outline

> Executive Summary (one page or less)
> Background and History of the Organization
> Parameters of the Needs Assessment
> Procedures
>   Population of the assessment
>   Sampling plan
>   Methodology
>   Means of analysis
> Results
> Conclusions
>   Issues determined
>   Recommendations
>   Training
>   Nontraining

In the actual assessment, we want to spend a bit of time describing the nature of the organization, including some brief history or background of the problem area on which we're focusing. For example, if a new division is created within a company, we want to talk about development of that unit if our needs assessment is of that particular division. We do not want to go into a ten- or twenty-page discussion of the founding of the organization, or include any of the historical materials we might incorporate if we were doing an annual report or a history of the company. Some background, however, is important to comprehend the outcome of our needs assessment. If possible, consult with the person to whom the report is to be delivered on how much background and history is needed. She or he can tell you who might read the report and how much background and history is relevant.

The next two sections of the assessment are pretty much the same as the proposal in that we describe the parameters and topic areas, as well as the procedures that we used in the actual assessment. Where the proposal talked about what we were going to do, the needs assessment talks about what we actually did.

A key difference between the needs assessment and the needs-assessment proposal is that we have completed the assessment. Now we have actual results to present in one section of the paper. If we presented employees with an attitude survey, we would present the results of the attitude survey at this point in the document. This might be a description of all the questions with a breakdown of the employees by area, or some other demographic characteristic. Exhibit 5.3 presents a typical page of results produced from a needs assessment. This is hypothetical and does not represent any particular organization. As you can see from the exhibit, we have taken two attitude items and looked at the results from a gender perspective. We could look at age, area of employment, and length of employment just as easily as the gender view. We must decide what ways we want to look at the data collected and present all of the information. In the results section we do not draw conclusions, just present the facts. We would note that a greater percentage of the females valued training than the males.

In the next section, we describe what the result means in terms of any conclusions we might want to draw. It is in the conclusion section of our needs assessment that we can tell management what we would recommend based on the conclusions. For example, we might tell management that they have a problem with males in terms of training and that they need to demonstrate the value of training. In another example, we might have found that the attitudes of employees were very low with regard to communication within the organization. We might recommend on the basis of the attitude items that communication be improved. We would draw similar conclusions in other areas of our results so that management would have a clear picture of what the results mean.

We should incorporate alternative explanations for our results if we discover through the assessment that the results may be due to more than just employee attitudes. For example, we might know from interviews that some employees are unhappy with their salary and are negative toward the company, organizational communication, and every other aspect of the company. To report only the negative attitude toward communication would not give a clear set of results. Assessors need to shed as much light as they can on the issues.

Finally, we make recommendations based on our findings in two specific areas. We would recommend, where appropriate, training for groups of individuals in the corporation. We may, for example, recommend as a result of our employee attitude survey that all managers be given training in how to involve employees in participative management. We want to recommend categories of training in the needs assessment without listing each and every training topic.

Many times the results of our surveys and assessments prove that training may not be necessary, but that there are some recommen-

Exhibit 5.3 Attitudes toward Training

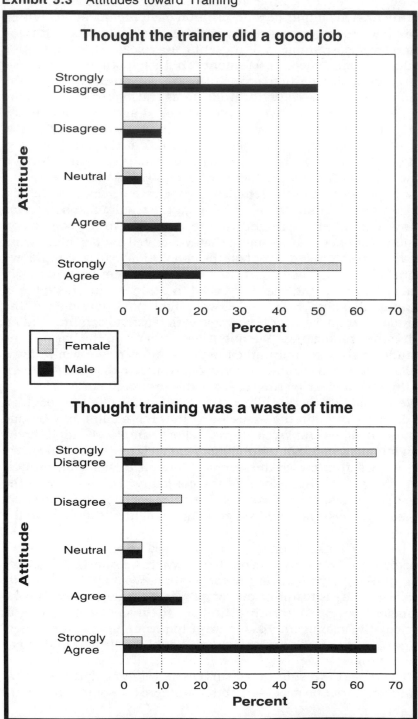

dations that could be made in nontraining areas. For example, we might find that a number of employees have personality characteristics and/or values that would suggest they don't belong in people-oriented jobs, but could do very well in other kinds of employment within the organization. This, then, would not be a training issue, but certainly could be a recommendation we would make to management regarding these employees. As we will discuss in later chapters, we do not want to overstep our competency by making recommendations when we are not qualified. We are not psychologists or counselors, so we limit our recommendations to areas of our expertise.

Thus, our needs assessment is a complete document, specifying the issues, the procedures, and the conclusions we would make relative to a specific audience and a specific assessment. We are now ready to present our document to our supervisor or contact person.

Training Proposals

Once the needs assessment is made, we may want to incorporate a training proposal in the document or develop a separate training proposal based on the needs assessment. If we choose the latter approach, we would want to develop a document following the outline in Exhibit 5.4. You will recall an earlier example in which we talked about a proposal to do a needs assessment, but the company chose to do its own assessment and then turned to us for training. To follow up on that example, we were given the company's needs-assessment document and the conclusions drawn from that assessment, and we were then asked to propose training on the basis of the needs assessment. In further interviews we developed the training proposal using the outline you see in Exhibit 5.4. We recommend this outline for any training proposal. Let's examine the various categories within the training proposal in more detail.

As with the other two types of proposals, we are firmly convinced that an executive summary provides an excellent overview, as well as a persuasive minidocument to convince the decision-makers of the need for the training. When time does not permit a full review of the entire document, the executive summary contains a cogent synopsis of what is being proposed.

All of the other topics outlined in Exhibit 5.4 do not necessarily have to be presented in that specific order. We recommend that a trainer put them in the order appropriate for the organization. When

Exhibit 5.4 Training Proposal Worksheet

> Executive Summary
> Target Audience for Training
> Title of Program
> Length of Program(s)
> Number of Sessions
> Objectives for Each Session
> Content Narrative for Each Session
> Teaching Strategies
> Teaching Material
> Audiovisual Equipment
> Evaluation Plan
> Proposed Follow-up

making a proposal to do training, you are guided by any needs assessment previously conducted by you or others and by your conversations with the person who will hire you to do the training (decision-maker). One hiring agent may want your proposal to stress goals and objectives and may not care about a/v materials. Adapting your training proposal to meet the needs found in the assessment and to reflect the views of the decision-maker are your guides for ordering the proposal.

At some point in the document there should be a discussion of the trainees: who they are, and the purpose for their attending the training program. It should go beyond simply stating all managers at the supervisory level or above are the trainees. There should be a discussion as to why these people need the training we are proposing. We want to anticipate questions like "Why all managers?" or "Why only the employees?"

Certainly the title of a program would be optional, although selecting the title may help motivate employees. If the title indicates that participants will be in a training program on participative management practices, they may not be as motivated as if they are going to be put in a participative interactive management (PIM) program (of course, you'd better define the jargon). It says the same thing, but may offer a little more pizzazz. The title, as well as the description, can be useful if the training programs are going to be voluntary rather than mandatory. Can you imagine employees giving up a day off to attend an all-day seminar on Affirmative

Action regulations? They might, however, come to a session on "Avoiding lawsuits; hiring and firing with new Affirmative Action guidelines."

The next two sections should incorporate the length of the program, as well as the number of sessions to accommodate the training. You may determine on the basis of your needs assessment and your program design that you need approximately twelve hours to develop a sound, listening-skills training package. Thus, the length has been determined, but you need to decide how the segments are going to be presented and the number of sessions. Would it be better to break up the twelve hours into two six-hour segments, four three-hour sessions, or three four-hour sessions? The resolution of these questions depends in a large measure on the content of the program, as well as the work schedules of the target participants in the training program. It may not be feasible to establish two six-hour training programs, but it might be feasible to offer four three-hour sessions spread over a 3-month period so that the trainees can adapt their own work schedules to the training program.

We believe that the proposal should include objectives for each training session, as well as a brief narrative of what will be covered within the session. We are not proposing that a complete description of the entire course and lesson plans be developed for your training proposal. The proposal should only give the manager enough information to decide whether it meets the needs assessment that has been conducted on the organization. Later, you will want to develop the complete program to ensure more effective training.

The next two sections talk about the strategies and materials that will be used for the training program. In other words, many managers want to know what teaching strategies will be used. For example, will the trainer offer a lot of participation or more of a straight lecture-discussion approach? From our discussion in chapter 3 of the adult learner, our bias on this issue leans heavily toward participation. What we're doing is giving the manager or decision-maker enough information to decide that this training is something which should be delivered.

Some discussion should be included of what audiovisual equipment will be necessary for two reasons. First, is such equipment available in the organization? Second, spelling out the audiovisual needs will give the decision-maker further information on the teaching strategy to be incorporated by trainers.

No other portion of a training proposal is as important as the evaluation plan. In chapter 9 we will discuss fully how one can go about evaluating the training program, but we need to underscore here that any training program should describe what evaluation will be used and how it will occur. Will the evaluation simply be a reaction to the training at the end of the sessions, or will there be some kind of on-the-job assessment of the training as it relates to employee participation and productivity? It's important that the evaluation plan be spelled out, particularly if it's going to occur long after the training program has been completed.

The final section, which is really a part of the evaluation, includes plans for a follow-up. Many times, managers and decision-makers balk at the training that is provided because it is like a shot in the arm: it helps for a while, but if there is no follow-up it has little lasting value. If we can incorporate some kind of follow-up to show that the training not only will be integrated, but also will be assessed periodically over six to twelve months, there is a greater likelihood that the training can be conducted.

We have thus described the type of training proposal that ought to be done whether you are an in-house trainer or an outside consultant. As we have suggested with the other two proposals, the training proposal is of greater importance for the outside consultant than it might be for the in-house trainer. It's a good exercise for the in-house trainer to develop such a proposal even though the decision may be made inside the training unit. This proposal becomes a viable way of assessing the effectiveness of a training program within an organization by having it on file, even though approval may not be necessary from corporate management.

Presenting Proposals

We have described, then, three basic types of proposals that a trainer has to make on the job. We would like to talk a little bit about some of the characteristics of presenting the proposals without going into a complete discussion of written style or how to make oral presentations. We will touch on who the audience might be, how the proposals might be presented, and what the content might be.

Who should hear or read the training proposal? If you are working inside the organization, your immediate supervisor may be the appropriate audience for any of the three proposals. Sometimes this will be the vice-president of human resources; or, you may report directly to the president or CEO. If you are an outside consultant, the person who should receive the proposal is the one who requested you submit the proposal in the first place.

The reason this is a significant issue is that many times we do proposals only to discover that one of the problems within the organization is the very person who has requested the proposal in the first place. We have an ethical obligation to return the report with recommendations to the person who requested it, rather than to go over the head of that individual, either to a higher level of management or to a board of directors. If, in fact, the manager who requested the proposal is ineffective, that is something that person's supervisor will have to discover and deal with, rather than using our report as a basis for such information. We are presenting our proposal to the person who requested it, rather than someone we personally might think would benefit most from it. That's not to say that the person who requests it might not want us to give the proposal in written or oral form to others. In essence, we are saying that the proprietary rights of the assessment or proposal belong to the person who requested it.

For example, you may be asked by a corporate CEO to assess his or her organization. After interviews with employees, clients, managers, and the board of directors, you discover the CEO is a problem. You must still give your report to the CEO. If you are on good terms with the CEO, you can direct pointed issues to him or her.

Should the report be in oral or written form? Here there is no right or wrong answer, but only what is appropriate. If a written report is requested (or not rejected), it probably should be put in writing, even if an oral report is made in the first place. We are convinced that an oral report can be very effective but, like the executive summary, a written report is something that our manager or hiring agent could go back and look at in order to make final decisions. So, what are we saying? We are saying make the oral report only if that is what management has requested. If the door is left open, then certainly do an oral report followed by a written proposal like the ones we have suggested in the three different outlines. We can be very effective orally, but a written report provides good follow-up.

How should the reports be structured? We have offered sample structures for the three different types of reports. These are not cast in concrete, but are suggestions as you begin to develop proposals. They seem to be fairly standard and cover the essential information that would be requested by management or a decision-maker, in the case of an outside consultant.

The final question we need to consider is, what should the content of the various proposals be? We've tried to stress all along that when we make proposals, we keep the specific information limited. We do not believe that you should reveal all of your attitude items, for example, in a proposal to do a needs assessment, or all of the sampling procedures in great detail. Perhaps we're being somewhat paranoid here, but we are convinced that if it's your proposal it ought to remain as such and not be something done for others so that they might then go ahead and do the work without you. This is probably a bigger problem for the outside consultant, because we know of a number of cases where organizations have requested proposals only to decide that they would do the needs assessment and/or training in-house, and then incorporated what was submitted as proposals by outside bidding agencies. Certainly this is not ethical, but it would appear to be a practice used by some organizations. Therefore, it's essential, whether you are working in-house or are earning a fee for service, that you provide enough information to get the proposal accepted, but not so much information that the proposal could stand alone without your specific help.

In the needs assessment, we are convinced that you should provide as much information as you possibly can, keeping in mind the issues we described in chapter 4 with regard to the confidentiality of the people who are interviewed or surveyed. You have an obligation to avoid revealing the identity of individuals if the descriptions of their job titles would, in fact, reveal who they are. For example, if there are three employees within a division, each one varying in age by 20 years and by number of years within the organization, it wouldn't take very long for someone to figure out who the three individuals were and what their opinions are. Certainly you would be violating their confidentiality in providing that kind of detail. It is important in the needs assessment that the reader understand the basis for any results and conclusions you might draw. While we have yet to discuss ethics, we do want to be careful in how we draw conclusions based on our needs assessment findings. It's very easy to say that the employees of X division were unanimous in their dislike for a particular employment practice, only to discover that only three of the ten employees filled out the questionnaire. This kind of information would certainly bias the results and conclusions we could draw.

Summary

What we have tried to do in this chapter is to spell out for you the types of proposals that trainers are often called upon to make, as well as to describe how you might present a needs assessment. We have talked about the proposal to do a needs assessment, the needs assessment, and the training proposal. We've also talked about who you should address your proposal to and the format in which the proposal ought to be presented. In the next chapter we will talk specifically about how to design the training program that you have discovered was needed on the basis of your needs assessment.

Designing Training Programs

Objectives

This chapter will help you

- ▶ recognize ways to develop training programs that support organizational goals
- ▶ identify ways to implement objectives to meet these goals
- ▶ understand the elements involved in designing a training model
- ▶ design training programs that meet multiple clients' needs

Introduction

The previous chapters described conducting and presenting the needs assessment. Once the needs assessment has been conducted and the data have been analyzed and presented to appropriate people, the trainer is ready to design programs to address these needs. A "vocational danger" in the training profession is the temptation to do "art for art's sake." It is important to remember that rather than falling in love with our favorite topics or our favorite methods and techniques, we need to stick to the goals and objectives established through our needs analysis. Training programs ultimately are evaluated on the basis of how much they help organizations meet goals and objectives.

Goal Development

Goals are the long-term outcomes we hope to accomplish. Because they are long-term, they tend to be relatively vague and difficult to measure. An example of a long-term goal for a company is increased profits; other examples are greater productivity from employees, increased morale, more accuracy and, ultimately, customer satisfaction. Sometimes, goals such as these can be translated into more specific terms. For example, the goal of increased profits can be translated into dollars or percentages. Goals also can be put in time frames, such as one month or one year. Customer satisfaction can be measured by customer comments and other forms of feedback and, ultimately, repeat business. Other goals, such as increased morale, are much more difficult to describe in tangible terms. Nevertheless, the management of every organization has an idea of what it means by these goals—for example, morale may be measured by how willingly employees will learn each other's jobs, how quickly they will fill in for a coworker who is absent, or how they rate the department or firm on a survey questionnaire. Because of limitations in both time and budget, and because of the degree of competition among organizational departments for these resources, the training department must make sure that everyone in the organization sees how the training programs contribute to organizational goals.

This may sound simpler than it really is. Largely because of time constraints and also because of organizational politics, organizational goals as top management identifies them may be difficult for the trainer to identify. For example, top management's official, publicized goals may be to provide excellence and quality. But what does this mean in practical terms? In a sense, this is a marketing issue. Just as a marketing person must know the customer's goals before he or she can sell a product, so must the trainer know the goals of top management. Ideally, this information would reach the trainer through the hierarchy. In other words, the trainer's boss would get information about company goals through his or her own boss, and so on. In reality, however, there are often big gaps in the formal communication system. These gaps mean that the trainer may not know the specific, day-to-day details that top management defines as excellence or quality. Because of these gaps, the trainer must have access to the *informal* network within the organization. The informal network is the relationships among people. Usually, these relationships do not follow the pattern of the formal chain of command as indicated by such things as organizational charts. Instead, informal relationships are based on common interest, shared experiences, friendships, and other kinds of circumstances beyond the actual work environment. While the formal chain of command indicates the way things are supposed to be, the informal system represents the way things *are*. Through such informal sources as the grapevine, social visits, or casual remarks made by someone in the car pool, the trainer may learn the specifics of what top management means by its long-term goals. In one firm, for example, the president's idea of excellence was employees conforming to official standards, while in another firm the president wanted suggestions from workers at all levels. The trainer must get both formal and informal communication about top management's goals.

Top managers are not the only ones with goals. Every department has its own goals, which should be based on organizational goals. Departmental goals tend to be a little more specific than organizational goals. For example, the marketing department's goals might be to save money in advertising, to find innovative ways to sell new products, or to increase the creativity of its employees. In a manufacturing firm, the goals of the assembly line might be to increase the productivity of each employee or to decrease turnover. In designing training programs, the trainer must become very familiar with the department's goals.

As organizations become more team oriented, and as teams become more self-directed, each team within a department also has its own specific goals. For example, a team of manufacturing specialists working on the assembly line may hire its own coworkers. The objective of team members may be to improve their own interviewing skills or to establish uniform criteria with which to select the best applicants. Sometimes, teams consist of employees from two or more departments. A goal of such a team may be, for example, establishing an organization-wide mentoring program for high-potential employees. The trainer must be clear about the goals of different teams within and among departments.

In addition, individual employees have their own goals and the trainer must learn what these goals are. Just as department or team goals sometimes may differ from—and even conflict with—organizational goals, employee goals may differ from department or team goals. An employee may want shorter hours and more interesting work, while the department manager may want longer shifts and more routine steps, and the team wants more training for job rotation. Some employees may be interested in career opportunities, while others may simply want to "put in their time." The trainer must coordinate employee goals with team, department, and organization goals.

The training department itself, and teams within the department, also have their own goals. Usually the director of training reports to a vice-president, either of personnel or human resource development, or of a related area. Presumably, the vice-president is active in the organizational goal-setting at the top level. Through this formal channel—and through the informal channels discussed earlier—the training department is aware of organizational goals. This department, however, really is a liaison, both between top management and all other departments and among individual departments and teams. The training department also has its own teams, and must do liaison work among these teams as well. This liaison, or linking, role exists because training is the department that knows the most about everyone else's needs. In addition to addressing top management goals, the training department needs to mesh the goals of each department and team within the firm.

Once the training department is familiar with organizational goals from the top and throughout the company, priorities need to be reestablished. Budgetary and time constraints make it impossible to do everything. Instead, only a certain number of goals will be accomplished at any given time. Needs that are identified through the assessment process help indicate which goals are most important. Sometimes, the training department makes these decisions. Often, however, training must check with top management to get input about priorities. For example, suppose the employees needed training both in using new equipment and in dealing with customers, but time and money allowed for only one kind of training in the next six months. The trainer probably would check with management before choosing which program to schedule first.

By using the needs assessment data as a way of determining which goals need to be met, the trainer is better able to establish priorities. As an example, suppose that one of the company goals is to improve customer reaction to the firm and its products. Suppose that on the level of the marketing department, the goal is to improve customer relations over the telephone. Without knowing anything about needs, it might appear appropriate for the training department to design a course in telephone courtesy. However, what if the needs assessment indicated problems in the areas of time management, bookkeeping, motivation, and writing skills? Would a telephone courtesy program be appropriate under these circumstances? Of course it would not. Suppose, however, that the needs assessment showed weaknesses in the areas of written communication, verbal communication, complaints about telephone clerks, or ways for the clerks to deal with their own anger. In this case, a telephone courtesy program would indeed be appropriate. Based on the other issues brought up in the needs assessment, such a program might include such topics as how to deal with one's own anger and with a customer's anger. The needs assessment, then, helps the trainer identify the order in which larger goals are to be addressed.

No matter how well the trainer determines what appear to be appropriate goals for a training program, he or she will not be very successful without getting input from appropriate people within the firm. It is important to remember that the training department provides a service for the entire organization. In this sense, people throughout the firm are "clients" of the training department. Just as a store owner would not tell a customer what style of clothes to wear, the trainer cannot dictate what kinds of programs employees need. Instead, the trainer needs to cooperate with the clients, win their support, learn their perceptions of what issues must be addressed, identify what goals the client wants to accomplish, and coordinate all this information with company goals and the needs assessment. Sometimes, the trainer has to sell a need to employees, if top management perceives a need but employees do not. For example, management may think that employees need to improve their letter-writing skills, but employees think the problem is that company policy is too strict about customers' returning merchandise. The trainer is the link between management and employees, and must sell what management perceives as a need and what employees perceive as the problem. Another consideration is that many employees may resist the idea of suggesting to the trainer what goals to meet. "That's your job," they may say. All the trainer can do is provide the opportunity for input when it comes to developing goals.

Another consideration is that goals will later serve as ways to measure the effectiveness of a training program. As stated previously, because goals often are long-term and difficult to measure, they need to be translated into more specific measures that are observable; these measures are called objectives.

Objectives Development

Objectives cannot be set until goals are clearly defined. Once goals are defined, developed, and agreed upon, the trainer is ready to set specific, measurable objectives. Objectives are the specific steps to be taken to accomplish a goal. Suppose, for example, that the goal is to increase employee productivity on the assembly line. First, the goal has to be put in more specific terms. "Increased productivity" might mean that instead of producing ten tools per hour, an employee would produce thirteen. Before objectives can be set, the trainer must determine what would be required before employees could produce a greater number of tools. If assembly line equipment had to be replaced, for example, this would not call for a training program at all. If, however, lower productivity was due to such causes as workers' unfamiliarity with assembly methods, lack of skill in using equipment, problems in understanding instructions, or other trainable deficiencies, then appropriate steps could be taken in a training program. Once the problems are identified, the trainer still needs to find out specifics before he or she can set objectives. In our example, the trainer may learn that increased productivity requires workers to improve their skills on some of the equipment and to be trained in following instructions more carefully. The trainer would now be ready to set specific objectives. They might be:

1. Test employees' skills at machine X.
2. Test employees' abilities to follow various kinds of instructions.
3. Identify appropriate steps for operating machine X.
4. Identify problem areas in terms of employees' abilities to follow instructions.
5. Teach employees specific ways to run machine X.
6. Teach employees how to follow instructions more effectively.

With these six objectives in mind, the trainer has a clear idea of what materials to include, what testing procedures to use, and what content to teach. The trainer knows, for example, that the subject of following instructions probably will be more cognitive—that is, informational and requiring understanding—while the topic of running machine X also might require hands-on experience.

Given this example, you can see that the trainer still has research to do even after the needs assessment has been done. The task of setting objectives is even more difficult for such goals as increasing employee morale. One reason this is more difficult is that in the case of employee morale, it is not only employees who have to learn something. It may be, for example, that employee morale is low because of things that management is doing or not doing. If this were the case, managers, as well as employees, would need training. Objectives for the managers might include:

1. How to interpret employee behavior.
2. How to give and take feedback.
3. How to motivate employees.
4. How to deal with personality conflicts.

The objectives for employees might include:

1. How to communicate with your boss.
2. How to deal with coworkers.
3. How to make constructive suggestions at work.
4. How to deal with personality conflicts.

Notice, however, that if the real cause of low morale was low pay, these objectives would not address the issue at all. The trainer's job is to make sure that the real issues are identified. The trainer then has to make sure that the objectives are appropriate to reaching the goal—that is, to solving the problems or filling the real need. Obviously, the trainer must have a great deal of credibility with both management and employees in order to help both groups identify the real issues. Individuals often do not like to find out that they are "wrong" about what they think the problem is. However, the trainer must stick to issues—that is, the symptoms—rather than become enmeshed in who is "right." Perhaps one of the hardest things about the trainer's job is identifying the real problem. As an example, let's look at a situation in a firm for which one of the authors consulted. The production department and marketing department had many conflicts, and each thought the other was at fault. Production blamed marketing for "selling products we don't have the capacity to make," and marketing blamed production for "preventing us from selling to eager customers." When the consultant pursued the symptoms in depth, she recognized that the real problem had little to do with the two departments. Instead, top management was unclear about its priorities, and the confusion was indirectly passed down to the individual departments. The solution in this case was not training for the departments, but goal-clarifying sessions for top management. An experienced trainer can help everyone find the actual problems and needs within an organization.

As with goal development, it is important to include others in setting objectives. Because the trainees and the departments are your clients, you have to make sure they agree about objectives in order to make your programs effective. In addition to getting valid input about what your clients want, the process of including them in setting objectives helps make them more receptive to the programs you design and deliver. People feel committed to ideas and programs about which they have some say. The trainer accomplishes at least two things by getting input: first, people appreciate becoming involved and will be more willing to cooperate; second, employees' input often adds dimensions the trainer may otherwise miss. Once goals and specific objectives are developed, the trainer is ready to select training models.

Training Models

A training model is a specific set of methods for teaching. Because the teaching we are dealing with here involves adults learning about something at work, several issues must be considered before the trainer can choose the most effective model.

Trainees' Abilities

While the needs assessment gives the trainer a relatively clear picture of what department needs are, actual training programs must deal with individuals. Different employees, even in the same department, have different levels of skill, interest, experience, and ability. To make a training program effective, you must first find out how much each employee already knows, how motivated he or she is to learn more, and what exactly he or she needs to learn.

Suppose, for example, your needs assessment made clear that the secretaries at Company X needed training in using word processors. It would be unrealistic for you simply to design a program on the basis of state-of-the-art technology and present this program to the entire secretarial staff. Several of the secretaries may already know how to use word processors. Of those who do not know, some may learn very quickly while others learn more slowly. Still another group may resist the whole idea of word processors—a not-uncommon event. Your job would be to identify the needs of the individual secretaries and adapt the program accordingly.

How do you find out how much skill, information, ability, or motivation an individual employee has? Such things as physical skills may be measured by physical tests. For example, if you want to find out how well an ironworker can tie rebar steel, provide the employee with the necessary materials and see how good a job is done in how much time. To find how much an employee knows about something, you may use various kinds of questionnaires. For example, if you wanted to ask the ironworker how well he or she understood tying rebar, you could ask questions that called for written or spoken answers. Recognize, however, that a big difference exists between the employee's understanding about how to do a job and the employee's ability to do the job.

To learn about an employee's motivation—that is, about his or her interests in learning more about the job—no foolproof method really exists. Often, past performance is a clue as to how an employee will behave in the future. However, because people continually grow and change, it would be unfair to assume that, because of things they failed to do at one time, employees were not motivated. Various psychometric tests exist to measure such things as motivation, but these must be viewed with caution because motivation is such a difficult thing to measure. In one company, for example, employees in the sales department appeared to be unmotivated until a new trainer came to the firm. The trainer used her new position as a chance to ask lots of questions, and she discovered that the salespersons felt discouraged by the fact that they never received feedback about how their weekly sales compared to those of other firms. Once the manager learned about this problem, he was able to motivate the employees by providing needed information. What really matters to trainers is that employees care enough to try to learn something from the program. The trainer can contribute a great deal to the enthusiasm of the trainees. This enthusiasm can come from the setting, the teaching style, and other issues discussed below.

The Training Setting

What can a trainer do to help make participants eager to learn? While the particulars will vary with each group and each topic, certain things need to be considered. The first is that as adult learners, employees need hands-on experience as well as information. This experiential approach is relatively easy when you are teaching a physical skill. If an employee is learning how to run a forklift, for example, you could easily schedule time for the employee to practice with an experienced operator.

If you are teaching such things as selling skills, interpersonal skills, or how to do performance appraisals, however, you need to use your imagination to create realistic experiences for the trainee. One successful method of doing this is using role-plays. In a role-play, the trainee first learns the specific behaviors or skills that constitute what is to be learned. After having learned about these skills—that is, learning how they should be performed—the trainee will act out the part of the salesperson or the manager and practice performing these skills. For example, suppose trainees learned about giving performance appraisals. The first step probably would be to inform trainees about how to do appraisals: EEO requirements, effective ways to give feedback, and other cognitive knowledge. The role-play step would allow trainees to practice what they learned and actually to experience talking to someone about his or her job performance. The experience makes the cognitive information more meaningful. In addition, the practice allows the trainee to improve at the skill. Another trainee or the trainer would play the role of customer or employee.

At the end of the role-play, the trainee would receive feedback in various forms. The trainer would point out the ways in which the trainee's performance was effective and ways in which the trainee could improve. Notice the positive focus of the feedback: instead of criticism, the trainee receives suggestions for doing better. For example, in many companies, employees receive criticism when they make mistakes. The manager may say such things as "These numbers were incorrect," "The report was late," or other negative comments. A more positive and effective way to correct errors is to identify what is done well, and then show the employee how the performance can be even better. The trainer can set the example by using such phrases as "Most of this report is well done. To be more accurate, however, these numbers will have to be changed," or "I appreciate getting the report from you. It would have been more useful, however, if I had received it last Wednesday." Another source of feedback may be other trainees within the group. Trainees learn from watching each other as well as from watching the trainer. They also learn how to give feedback to and get feedback from their peers. Another powerful source of feedback is videotape. When trainees see and hear themselves perform, they have a chance to experience themselves the way others do. Trainers often sit with the trainees to watch the video-tapes and to highlight certain aspects of the trainees' behavior. Through both the practice itself and the various forms of feedback, trainees learn a great deal from experience when it supplements what they have learned about the subject.

Comfort Level

Another consideration is how to determine when trainees feel comfortable enough to perform, automatically, what they have learned. When a trainee is able to perform a skill well without having to think about it too much, he or she may be said to have reached a "comfort level" with that skill. You can easily see the advantages to a company when employees have reached their comfort levels in a variety of skills. For example, consider a salesclerk in a department store. While learning about the job, the clerk will have many questions, first about company procedure and then about the technicalities of running the computerized cash register. The clerk's learning process costs the company in terms of time. Once the clerk reaches a comfort level with the new job duties, his or her performance will be less costly in terms of time or errors.

Time Frame

Trainers must determine the time frame in which to structure training sessions. For example, courses may be presented in all-day sessions, half-day sessions, two-hour blocks, week-long ses-sions, or anything else that seems appropriate. There is no general policy about time frames. There are, however, several things to consider. First, information is more easily learned if it is presented in relatively short rather than long blocks of time. At the same time, however, a certain amount of continuous practice is necessary before a trainee can learn a new skill. The trainer must decide what the proper balance is, depending on what is being taught and who is learning. If managers are learning about new ways to motivate employees, a one- or two-day session might be appropriate for them, if this time frame would allow for discussions, exercises, and other activities. Because they have some experience, managers in this case would be learning specific tools rather than an entirely new area of information. Suppose, however, that the trainees were new construction workers. They would have a great deal to learn in terms of both information and skills. This would require an extended learning period. On-the-job training might be supplemented by short intensive sessions focusing on specific skills. The trainer's job is to use time frames that match the needs and the situation.

Teaching Styles

Trainers have a variety of styles from which to choose. One of the standbys is the lecture method, so common in college, in which the trainer conveys information to trainees while they take notes. This method is useful in very large groups and in situations where the information is not tied to specific behaviors; for example, a large group of employees may benefit from a lecture about changes in insurance benefits at work. They need the information, and they do not need to practice anything related to it.

For on-the-job skills, however, lectures are ineffective. As discussed in the chapter about adult learners, lectures do not work well with adults. In addition, lectures alone do not give trainees a chance to practice or experience what they have learned. Trainers should limit lectures as much as possible.

Role-plays.   As discussed previously, role-plays give trainees a chance to practice what they have learned and to get feedback about their performance. Employees often are self-conscious about role-plays, at least until they get started. Often, the trainer may want to pick trainees who are outgoing and willing to be the first ones.

Assessment centers.   In these experiences, the trainer creates a simulated situation where trainees act as they would at work. For management training, the assessment center event might include a stack of phone messages, and the trainee would set priorities in terms of what he or she does about each message at that moment. The purposes are to give trainees real-life experience and to allow them to get feedback about their decisions and actions.

What is important about teaching styles is that trainers must use whatever methods work with each group. Some trainees want to be told what to do, while others like to have input during training sessions, and still others like to interact with other trainees as well as with the trainer. Training is most effective when the methods fit the group.

Application to the Job

As we said at the beginning of this chapter, training programs are evaluated according to how well they meet organizational needs and how much they help organizations reach goals. This means that all the trainers' clients evaluate programs in terms of their own understanding of problems.

Top management will evaluate training programs by the bottom line: Do employees work more efficiently, meet company standards, and accomplish long-term goals? Are our customers more satisfied and are they buying more? Mid-level managers will measure training programs by how well their departmental goals are met; for example, do employees work better together, are they skilled at using new equipment, does their work make the manager look good? Employees themselves will measure training programs by how much they can apply to work; that is, did they learn what they needed to, do they have new skills, can they deal with co-workers and bosses more effectively?

The training department, and individual trainers, also will be evaluated according to how professionally they treat their clients. Do they respect confidentiality? Do they stick to work-related issues and avoid getting personal? Do they treat trainees with respect and enthusiasm? The training department is evaluated by how well it meets others' needs.

Summary

The design of a training program must reflect the results of the needs assessment. Another way of saying this is that the training program and, ultimately, the training department will be evaluated according to how well they meet actual company needs.

The design must include goal development, which means that the program will help carry out one or more long-term goals of the organization. This task is difficult, because of both the vagueness of long-term goals and the number of interpretations of these goals. Identifying numerous clients and setting priorities are major responsibilities of the trainer.

Program design also includes objectives development, through which the trainer identifies the specific results that will come from a program. Each result must relate to, and must be presented as relating to, desired goals.

In designing a program, the trainer establishes a training model of specific methods of teaching. The training model considers trainees' abilities, an appropriate setting, a comfort level, a time frame, and teaching styles.

The trainer must always remember that management's evaluation of programs will be based on how applicable the results are to the job, and what the effect is on customer satisfaction and the bottom line.

| Conducting Training Programs | Chapter 7 |

Conducting Training Programs

Chapter 7

Objectives

This chapter will help you

- ► understand concerns that must be addressed when conducting training sessions
- ► recognize which kinds of settings are most effective for different kinds of training
- ► identify formats that are most appropriate for specific training needs
- ► understand the strengths and weaknesses of team teaching

Introduction

After identifying and presenting the organization's needs and having designed the appropriate programs, it is time to conduct a training session. Remember that the key to whether a training program is successful is how much it improves employee performance on the job. When conducting a training program, the delivery must be as useful and relevant as the content.

Initial Concerns

The actual training session is the moment of truth for the trainer. Will the participants be eager to attend the session? Will their objectives match those we have set? Will they learn what the program is designed to teach them? How much of what they learn will they be able to remember and use on the job? As a trainer, you naturally will be concerned about these issues.

Participants' motivation also will be a concern to the trainer. The trainer's job, however, is not to motivate the trainee. Motivation comes from within individuals and cannot be imposed upon them from the outside. What the trainer can do is create an environment that allows trainees to motivate themselves. One element of this environment is to include participants in goal setting for the training session. While you, as a trainer, have identified general goals through the needs assessment, it would be wise to get participants to state their specific goals for each session. One reason is to help the trainees feel included in determining the direction of the program; another reason is to help find out what interests and needs the individual trainees have. The more these needs can be addressed during the session, the more participants will motivate themselves to learn, remember, and use the information and skills they acquire. Both of the authors of this text begin their workshops by asking participants to identify, briefly, their goals for the session. One word of caution is in order, however: If you ask for participants' goals, be sure to address these goals during the workshop. Otherwise you will have built up participants' expectations and then disappointed them.

At the same time, remember to consider the objectives of individual managers whose employees are being trained. While the needs assessment gives an accurate picture of organizational issues, individual managers may differ in which issues they emphasize. Suppose that the assessment indicated a company-wide need for training in time management, computer literacy, and performance appraisals. You still need to find out which of these skills is most important to the specific department with which you are dealing. Remember that each manager will evaluate the effectiveness of the training program according to his or her own standards.

Another way to help trainees motivate themselves is to show them the ways in which they will benefit from what they are going to learn. By believing that the training session will lead to outcomes they expect, the trainees are more likely to learn and remember what is taught.

Environmental Considerations

As a trainer, your training sessions should be conducted in ways that help participants remember and use information and skills. One way to do this is to make the training session resemble the actual job situation as closely as possible.

Suppose you are training participants for a job that involves answering numerous phone calls in a noisy, high-pressure atmosphere. At the presentation stage—when discussing the skills participants need—a quiet setting would be reasonable. When the participants practice these skills, however, a room full of ringing telephones, loud voices, and noisy copy machines would be more realistic. Practicing the new skills in a setting that closely resembles work enables participants to transfer these skills more quickly to the job.

Two major types of training environments are on-site settings and off-site settings. Each has advantages and disadvantages in terms of how closely it resembles the actual work setting. Other considerations, however, help determine which type of environment is most appropriate.

On-Site Settings

On-site settings include various locations within the firm's office or plant. These settings are realistic, because they are in or near the actual places trainees work, and they avoid the costs of off-site locations. Several types of training are best suited for on-site locations. One is employee orientation, where new employees learn about company policy, individual job responsibilities, relationships between managers and employees, career opportunities, and similar topics. Because the purpose of orientation is to help the new employee become familiar with the organization, on-site training enhances this process.

Another method best suited for on-site locations is on-the-job training. Through this method, employees learn a job by doing it, and their learning may be guided by a trainer, an experienced employee, or both. The on-site location allows the trainee to learn many aspects of the job in addition to the specific job duties. For example, a server in a restaurant learns how to wait on tables by practicing and observing what other servers are doing. In addition to learning the specific skills of taking orders and serving food, the server also learns the type of manner to convey: the atmosphere may be elegant and formal, or casual and friendly. These behaviors are different from the specific duties of taking orders and serving food, but they are an integral part of these duties. The on-site setting speeds up the process of learning both the duties of a job and the general behaviors associated with these duties.

Job rotation is another training method well suited to on-site locations. In job rotation, the trainee performs a series of jobs, spending a predetermined period of time (several days to several years) on each job. The purpose is to give the trainee a broad view of the organization and the various ways the jobs and departments interrelate. Suppose a computer operator's training includes working in the accounting and sales departments; this experience would enable the operator to gear the work toward the needs of each department. Again, the on-site experience increases the trainee's familiarity with the job.

Another training method that is appropriate for on-site settings is coaching. Coaching is similar to performance appraisals in that an employee and his or her supervisor review the employee's performance strengths and weaknesses. Coaching goes beyond appraisals, however, because it focuses on the employee's future goals and steps toward these goals. Through the coaching process, a cashier in a grocery store might express interest in becoming a store manager. The boss then would help the cashier identify courses or other training steps leading to this goal. In the coaching process, the trainer's role usually is limited to helping supervisors coach their employees. Trainers themselves do not deal directly with employees in this process.

Career development, another on-site method, involves trainers who specialize in career planning. In career development, employees take diagnostic tests to identify their interests and skills. The career specialist, who is familiar with company jobs and with the skills and knowledge required for these jobs, helps employees set long-term goals for career development. As an example, John was a draftsperson for two years and he knew that to make any progress in the company, he should go back to school and become an engineer. However, he did not feel particularly committed to this idea. After taking several diagnostic tests and talking with his firm's career specialist, John realized that he wanted more opportunities to work with people than an engineering job would provide. John combined his experience and his new realizations, and became an architect for the same firm.

In addition to the specific training methods presented so far, workshops in any number of subjects may be held in company conference rooms or other on-site locations. These workshops usually take one-half day to two days, and are designed to address a number of needs within the organization. Managers' workshops may cover new management techniques, administrative assistants' workshops may cover time management and communication, and supervisors' workshops may cover ways to deal with problem employees. For in-house workshops, the trainer plays a major role: designing, presenting, and evaluating the sessions.

The main advantages of on-site locations are that they provide a realistic setting and are virtually cost-free. A main disadvantage is that because of the proximity to their departments, participants may too easily be called away from the training session to take care of day-to-day problems at work.

Off-Site Locations

Off-site locations include meeting rooms in hotels, university conference centers, or other facilities designed to provide this service. Off-site locations mean added expense, but their advantage is that they allow participants to focus on the issues at hand instead of worrying about work. While professional consultants and trainers use these kinds of facilities to hold public workshops, in-house trainers also use these facilities for various types of programs.

Perhaps the most common training method used in off-site locations is the workshop. For example, new supervisors may need a one-day workshop outlining their new responsibilities and ways to carry out their new duties. The trainer may use a meeting room in a nearby hotel to get the supervisors away from the office so they are not available for phone calls or other interruptions.

Another type of training method that works well in off-site locations is programmed instruction, where trainees use texts to learn at their own rates. For example, a new salesperson may use programmed texts to learn the steps involved in selling. Pretests included in the text would allow the salesperson to identify those areas he or she already knew and could therefore skip.

Closely related to programmed instruction is computer-assisted learning. The interactive nature of a computer program—that is, the way trainees get "right" or "wrong" responses from the computer—gives trainees immediate feedback and speeds up the learning process. In addition, computers can provide simulated experience, as in driver education. For both programmed and computer-assisted instruction, companies must weigh the costs of developing programs against the benefits derived in terms of time saved and accuracy of learning.

One problem with off-site locations, in addition to the cost, is the possibility that ideas and skills learned in training sessions will not be transferred to the work situation. One firm held off-site training in word processing; the employees learned word-processing skills and appeared ready to use these skills at work. The office environment, however, was different from that of the workshop. In the office, employees had to deal with phone calls, noisy machines, interruptions, and a generally fast-paced atmosphere. Their word-processing skills appeared dramatically lower at work than in the training session. A more effective training environment would include the noise and distractions, making it possible for trainees to learn and practice under more realistic conditions. To avoid this problem, trainers must make their sessions as realistic as possible, using methods described in the next section, "Training Formats."

Whether trainers use on-site or off-site locations, the environment must help, rather than hinder, trainee learning. The temperature of the room should be comfortably cool, to help trainees remain alert. Acoustics should allow everyone to hear and be heard, to provide active participation. All slides, flip-charts, transparencies, and other visual aids should be easily accessible to everyone. Ironically, if the room setting is appropriate, no one will notice— only uncomfortable aspects of a room seem to stand out! Make the physical environment unnoticeable by making it conducive to learning.

Training Formats

The content of a training session—that is, what the session is about—is only part of the training package. The rest is process— how the content is delivered. While the content of a training session ultimately is the bottom line, the process of delivery determines how receptive trainees are and how quickly, and how well, they learn the content.

Lecture

The lecture is a traditional training method, but not necessarily the best one. Lectures are useful when the main purpose of training is to convey information. If a company wants to inform employees about changes in health-care benefits, a lecture would be an appropriate way to explain the changes. Lectures also are useful for large groups. If the company decides, for example, to explain the health-care benefits to all five hundred employees at one time, a lecture in a large auditorium would work. But when the purposes of a training session go beyond simply informing or trying to reach a large audience, the lecture is not the most effective method.

One shortcoming of the lecture is that it is one-way communication. The trainer talks, and the trainees listen—and often are not likely to ask questions, especially in large groups. Without verbal feedback, the trainer cannot tell whether he or she is coming across effectively. Even worse, the trainees do not have a chance to find out if they are learning what the trainer wants them to learn. As an example, a trainer in a medium-sized firm chose the lecture method to teach five hundred employees how to handle their time cards on the new computerized system. The unfortunate result was close to five hundred versions of the "correct" way to deal with the time cards. The trainer had to use other methods not only to teach employees the correct way, but also to undo their mistaken ideas about the correct way.

Another problem with the lecture is that its one-way nature conveys a negative, top-down message to trainees. This message says, "I'm the know-it-all trainer, and you're just a lowly trainee." Regardless of the contents the trainer wants to convey, lectures tend to create resistance among trainees because of the inequality of positions. In a technical firm, an experienced trainer who was new to the company used the lecture method to explain new software options to computer specialists. The specialists reacted in several negative ways, ranging from passive nonlistening to loud disagreements. Investigation indicated that the computer specialists were reacting more to the new trainer's "know-it-all approach" than to the information the trainer tried to convey.

The lecture method also is limited by its reliance on verbal skills. In a trucking company, a trainer spent two hours lecturing to the mechanics about ways to use new equipment. Because they were more oriented to physical application than to abstract verbal explanations, the mechanics got very little out of the lecture. They started learning about the equipment only after an experienced mechanic physically helped them use it. An unintended negative outcome of the lecture was that the mechanics felt "put down" by the verbally-oriented trainer.

Another shortcoming of the lecture is that it is not easily transferable to the job. Trainees may understand the concepts presented in a lecture, but still not be able to perform the related skills. A common problem in management development programs is that even though managers eventually understand the importance of praising employees, often they still do not actually praise their employees at work. Lectures may take care of the cognitive—that is, the conceptual or understanding—aspect of learning, but they do not address the actual performance.

The lecture also is limited by the fact that it does not deal with individual differences among trainees. In a hospital, a trainer lectured to head nurses, radiology supervisors, head pharmacists, and other department supervisors about ways to handle conflicts among employees. Because it was designed to cover everyone, the lecture was too general to be useful to anyone. The trainees' backgrounds and personalities were different enough to warrant a specific, instead of a general, approach.

Another problem with the lecture method is that because it does not invite input from trainees, it does not capture or involve them. Without involvement, trainees often fail to buy into the content of a lecture. The managers of a small accounting firm wanted the support staff to change several of the procedures they followed. The trainer used the lecture method to present the changes, and the staff listened obediently. At work, however, the staff members kept forgetting the new procedures. Had they been more involved in identifying the need for changes or in designing the new procedures, instead of simply being told about them, the staff members might have supported the changes more enthusiastically.

The lecture method is useful for conveying information or dealing with large groups. It has major shortcomings, however, as a training format. Several alternative training formats, discussed in the following sections, are more effective in practice.

Discussions

One dynamic alternative to lectures is the discussion format, where trainees make comments, ask questions, and give examples. A big advantage to discussions is that they involve participants directly in the subject matter. By taking part, the trainees buy into the session more strongly than in straight lectures.

Often, the format may be primarily lecture with regular input from trainees. At a workshop for secretaries, the facilitator described key points involved in time management and then asked the trainees to describe situations that illustrated these points. One benefit of this method is that it uses examples that are meaningful to participants. The process of incorporating trainees' comments within a lecture, however, requires excellent facilitative skills on the part of the trainer; what individuals will say cannot be predicted. In addition, trainees often feel uncomfortable speaking, even from their chairs, to a large group.

Another way to get trainee input is to break the larger group into smaller subgroups. Trainees usually feel comfortable speaking in groups of four or five. At the workshop for secretaries, the facilitator had the trainees talk in small discussion groups about problems they have dealing with telephone calls. Everyone had something to say, because the small groups served as support systems. After a few minutes, the facilitator had one representative from each subgroup summarize the issues raised in that subgroup. Partly because of support from the subgroup, and partly because of some individuals' tendencies to be more outgoing, each subgroup was able to produce a representative who would speak to the entire group.

Whether they are done within the larger group or within smaller subgroups, discussions make training sessions lively. They help trainees get more out of the sessions by encouraging them to put more effort into them.

Case Studies

Case studies can add a lot to discussions by giving participants something specific, yet nonpersonal, to talk about. A case study describes actual problem situations in a company, using artificial names, and the problems relate to several points covered in training sessions. The problem situations are described, but no solutions are offered. The trainees read the case study and offer their own alternative solutions, based on what they have learned in training sessions.

The trainer may have everyone work on the case study alone, or may assign trainees to groups of two or three. In a workshop for furniture warehouse personnel, the trainees read a case study about problems in the warehouse of a computer company, and then discussed the case study in groups of three. Although the case study clearly reflected problems similar to those in the furniture warehouse, trainees felt more comfortable talking about the problems in some company other than their own. The necessary problems were addressed without anyone feeling put on the spot.

On one level, the case-study format gives trainees a chance to apply some of the principles that were covered in training sessions. On another level, small-group approaches to solving the case studies create lively interaction among trainees. Because the case-study problems do not single out any particular individual, trainees often feel more comfortable discussing them openly.

Role-Plays

Role-plays give trainees a chance to enact, rather than simply discuss, various responses to problem situations. One purpose of enacting these responses is to give the trainees practice at a skill presented by the trainer. Another is to allow the trainees to get feedback both from the trainer and from other participants about how their behavior came across. A third purpose is to give trainees experience at giving feedback to each other. Role-playing helps trainees learn by doing.

Role-plays combine spontaneity and planning. In one sense, they are spontaneous, because the trainees choose their own reactions, words, and body language. In another sense, role-plays are planned, because the trainees already know which behaviors they are supposed to act out. The trainer may design the role-play situations, or the trainees may create their own.

In a workshop for new supervisors, the trainees did not yet have enough experience to predict problems they were likely to encounter. The trainer designed problem situations for them, based on input from experienced managers. Once the situation was described to them, the trainees took turns playing the role of supervisor, while another trainee acted out the problem person role. The trainee playing supervisor reacted in whatever ways he or she thought were appropriate. The trainees' reactions were based partly on their own personalities and experience, and partly on what they had learned so far in the workshop. Once they enacted their responses, the other trainees shared their reactions to each other's responses. After all the trainees got feedback from each other, the trainer added a few comments and suggestions.

In another example, experienced managers acted out role-plays they designed for themselves. Each trainee had a specific situation he or she wanted help dealing with, so each trainee described the situation to the group. Another trainee played the part of the other person—as described by the trainee designing the role-play—and the manager played himself or herself. Again, behaviors were based partly on individual personalities and experiences and partly on what the managers had learned in the workshop. The trainees gave each other feedback, and the trainer added comments at the end. In this situation, trust and confidentiality among the trainees and with the trainer were crucial to the success of the role-plays, because of the individual nature of the problem situations.

Role-plays give participants hands-on experience with ideas presented in workshops. They also allow trainees to observe each other's behaviors and give each other feedback.

Games and Simulations

While role-plays help trainees deal with individual relationships, management games and simulations help trainees deal with the system-wide nature of their organizations. These games focus on the decisions managers make about financial, marketing, planning, communication, policy, and other issues. Using computers to identify long-term and system-wide outcomes, these games show managers the consequences of choices they make. Through simulations, trainees gain experience without having to suffer real-world results.

Games and simulations involve several teams of four to six trainees each. The trainer describes the nature of the simulated company, the types of products it produces and sells, and the economic and competitive environment in which it operates. Based on this information, each team defines its own company: its goals, objectives, organizational structure, controls, and procedures. The conditions of each team's company are identical, and trainees begin with a report of what these economic, financial, marketing, personnel, and other conditions are.

On a regular basis each team of trainees makes decisions for its simulated company. The "regularity" may be simulations of daily, weekly, monthly, or quarterly time frames. These decisions are processed on a computer, which prints out operating reports of outcomes based on the decisions. The process of making decisions and getting reports continues for a simulated year. Trainees usually have about thirty minutes to make decisions. "Winners" are determined according to net profit and such issues as return on investment, market share, personnel policies, and other factors that affect businesses.

At the end of the games and simulations, trainees receive feedback from each other, from the trainer, and from other specialists who have observed the activities. One aspect of the feedback focuses on content—that is, the specific decisions each team made and how those decisions affected the simulated company's situation. Another aspect of the feedback focuses on process: how the team went about making decisions, what degree of participation each team member had, how conflicts within each team were managed, and related issues. When decision-making sessions are videotaped, trainees can get an objective view of their own behavior.

Through games and simulations, managers gain realistic experience that closely parallels their day-to-day situations. By seeing the potential consequences of their behavior, the trainees easily can transfer their learning to the work setting.

Numerous training formats add dimensions to the learning process. When you conduct training sessions, choose the format that best suits your trainees, the material, and the organization.

Team Teaching

One way to pack a lot of information and variety into a training session is to use a multimedia approach in terms of trainers. Team teaching means that two or more trainers conduct a session together. This is different from serial teaching, where one trainer runs the session on Monday, and another trainer runs it on Wednesday. Team teaching means the trainers share the same session. In presenting information and interacting with trainees, they also interact with each other.

Two trainers, Joan and Al, conducted a communication session for department heads in a nonprofit organization. Joan began by pointing out several key communication principles. At a natural pause, Al added a few more points, sometimes looking at the trainees and sometimes looking at Joan. The variety of speakers and the dialogue added interest to the session.

One important aspect of team teaching is that the trainers build on what the other says and does. In the previous example, Al added similar information to Joan's discussion. Another way to build is to offer different views about the same topic. Later in the same example, Al presented ways to handle communication problems among office workers. After he described one specific way, Joan said, "Another way you might approach this is . . . ," giving a different perspective. In this situation, the trainers must be careful to focus on building, and not to appear as if they are disagreeing.

Another important aspect of team teaching is to use trainers who share both similarities and differences in their backgrounds. While the trainers must both be qualified in the same field, they need to offer different experiences to make an interesting team. Too much similarity between trainers will have a negative effect on trainees, who may feel that they are getting a hard sell. While it is important for the trainers to get along with each other, they also must be careful not to get so involved in each other's comments that they leave out the trainees.

In team teaching, the trainers can present variety that holds trainees' interest and can support each other in several ways. Careful planning and similar knowledge, on the one hand, and spontaneity and differences, on the other, can create a dynamic experience for trainees.

Summary

When you are ready to conduct the training session, you have a number of issues to consider about participants' needs, managers' expectations, the appropriate environment, the most suitable training format, and the usefulness of team teaching.

On site settings are best for employee orientation, on-the-job training, job rotation, coaching, career development, and related topics. Off-site settings work well for workshops, programmed instructions, and computer-assisted learning.

Training formats include lecture, discussions, case studies, role-plays, and games and simulations. Team teaching offers a multi-media option.

Remember that you have a number of good options from which to choose. Base your decisions on the nature of the trainees, the material to be covered, the managers' desired outcomes, and your needs assessment.

Using Audiovisual Aids

Objectives

This chapter will help you

- ► recognize the purposes for visual aids in training
- ► identify the types of visual aids
- ► understand the four rules for use of visual aids
- ► design appropriate visual aids for your material

Introduction

The often-quoted comment in public speaking is that a picture is worth a thousand words. If the picture is clear, can be seen by all, and relates to the message, the expression holds true. If not, you are better off using a thousand words. We have not forgotten a former student of ours who heard us talking about the value of the media, particularly the use of slides with an audiotape. For his demonstration, he decided to use four slide shows with four separate audio messages, all playing at the same time. Needless to say, his points got lost in the media presentation, and we certainly had a good example of noise pollution for the class to discuss. Unfortunately that was not the purpose of his message. In this chapter we would like to talk about the ways in which you can enhance your training material by using audiovisual materials. We will cover all of the technology that is available to you as a trainer, including the use of a computer.

As you recall from previous chapters, you have conducted the needs assessment and decided what programs you are going to present in your training sessions. Once you have designed the program, developed your objectives, and planned your lecture material, you can begin to think about and plan what audiovisual aids you will use to enhance the material that you plan to incorporate in training.

We hope that you will think of other ideas beyond the traditional audiovisual aids such as flip charts, chalkboards, films, slides, and overheads. We want you to think about magazine ads, Tinkertoy building blocks, and Play-Doh modeling clay, to name a few, as other perhaps more innovative ways to enhance your training. We have even seen trainers use trainees as live visual aids to make a point.

Now that we have aroused your interest in Play-Doh, we do not plan to write a definitive treatise on its use in training sessions. Rather, we would like to explore some of the traditional ways to enhance your training and then discuss, at least on an introductory level, some of the nontraditional ideas that we have found successful. If you choose to develop your skills in training beyond this introductory presentation, we would recommend two specific behaviors to you. First, you can read materials that are listed in our bibliography on audiovisual techniques and strategies. Second, you can take a course in instructional technology and development that might be available at a nearby college or university. Either way, you should go on and explore audiovisual materials in more depth than we can provide in this introductory chapter.

As an overview, we would like to talk first about the purposes of audiovisual aids, when you should use them and when you should not use them. We will then discuss each of the various types of audiovisual aids, when that specific aid is appropriate, and for what size group you should use it. We will conclude the chapter with a discussion of what we consider to be some of the nontraditional a/v (audiovisual) materials.

Purpose of A/V Materials

The purpose of visual aids is to enhance the message you are trying to get across to your trainees. If you are using audiovisual materials as a gimmick, it will certainly come across that way to your training audience. If you use too many of them, or inappropriate ones, that too will be perfectly clear. We have probably all heard stories about teachers who dress up in period costumes in order to teach history, as in dressing up as Shakespeare to talk about fifteenth-century England. This could be a very effective use of visual aids if we remember what was discussed rather than that the teacher dressed up as William Shakespeare. It is more important to make Shakespeare's *literature* come alive than Shakespeare himself.

There are a number of things that should guide you in answering the question, "Should I use a visual aid?" First and foremost, if the visual aid—a slide, a video, computer graphic, a handout—will enhance the basics of your training program, then you should certainly use it. If a picture can convey more than simply words, then you should consider the use of a/v materials. A series of slides showing the various components of a computer word-processing system could be far more effective than just talking about it. Finally, if you view the audiovisual aid as a way of helping the trainee remember the *content* of your training program rather than the way in which you used the visual aid, then you should consider incorporating audiovisuals into the training package. As we suggested earlier on developing training materials, and as we suggested at the beginning of this chapter, consider audiovisual aids only after you have developed the full course content. Go back over your training materials and decide what would be an appropriate place for the use of audiovisuals.

On the same score, there are a number of things you should keep in mind in regard to when it would be inappropriate to use visual aids. If you find that you have incorporated too many a/v materials like our student described in the beginning of this chapter, then it is time to back off and cut out some, if not all, of your a/v supplements. Too many aids can spoil the effectiveness of a sound training program.

You should also keep in mind how much time you have in order to prepare audiovisual materials. If your overheads are sloppy, if your videotape is poor quality, or your audiotape can't be heard, you are better off not using these poorly prepared materials. Remember, your image is at stake, in addition to the presentation of the training program. We don't know for certain that good visual aids will add that much to a training program, but we do know that poorly prepared a/v materials can detract from the overall effectiveness of our training.

Finally, you should not use visual aids if they are either scheduled at an inappropriate time or are inappropriate for the nature of the content. Showing a series of slides because it is time for diversion is not making effective use of a/v materials. We recall a colleague who used slides for a session on relaxation and stress. The trainees commented that the slides looked more like the trainer's vacation pictures than pictures designed to promote relaxation. Our colleague confessed they were right and he had learned the valuable lesson that these slides were inappropriate for this group. We are also reminded of a colleague who taught all of his classes by stringing together films and videotapes with little other material. Students confessed lots of sleep time and little learning.

We have but four simple basic rules that we subscribe to in the use of audiovisual aids in training programs. If these four general rules are kept in mind, use of a/v materials can be very effective.

Rule No. 1: Audiovisual aids should be confined to a single concept. For example, if you were to use an overhead you might want to focus on only one issue per overhead. You would certainly not want to cover the history of the theories of management all on one overhead or slide. The same principle applies to video—you would not want to play thirty minutes of tape on management principles when all you really wanted to discuss was leadership style. You would be far better off to play only an excerpt from the tape that confines discussion to the single concept. You might even want to create your own video or use live role-playing as the visual aid.

Looking at Exhibit 8.1, we can see an overhead that has lots of information but is cluttered with materials that, on the surface, do

Exhibit 8.1   Cluttered Overhead

Evaluation of Training

Cost	Status/Prestige
Feedback	Knowledge
Identify leaders	Improvement
Effectiveness	Remedial

Productivity

not relate well to each other. Are these factors of training evaluation or productivity? Does each item in the list have equal value? Only our trainer knows the relationship of the items on the overhead. In the second example, Exhibit 8.2, the trainer wants to remind the trainees of the two major types of training evaluation. In fact, a participant in the training program could probably figure out what was meant with this visual aid without any other notes from the training session. This overhead is straightforward and uncluttered.

Exhibit 8.2   Uncluttered Overhead

Major Types of Evaluation

1. Immediate questionnaire
2. Observation on job

Rule No. 2: Make sure that every member of your training audience can see and/or hear the audiovisual aid. If you are playing an audiotape, you should determine in advance that everyone, regardless of where they sit in the training room, can hear the material on the tape clearly. If you are using a micro tape recorder for an audience of 150, you had better make sure that you have a microphone or some other form of amplification so that all can hear the material. Showing 8 x 10 photographs to an audience of more than five or six would be another violation of this general rule. You would not pass around this book to show everybody the above exhibit. If all trainees cannot see it, or if they cannot hear it, you have made inappropriate use of your audiovisual aid.

Rule No. 3: Maintain control of your audiovisual. What does this mean? The beginning student in a public-speaking class perhaps is most guilty of violating this rule. When told to use visual aids, invariably a student will come with a series of pictures of his or her summer vacation. As the student progresses through the talk, the pictures begin circulating among fellow students with those at the beginning anxious to see each and every picture and those in the back of the room recognizing that they may never get to see them. If everybody cannot see the visual aid at the same time, you have lost control and you are better off not using the visual aid. The same student could have put the pictures on slides and thus maintained control of the visual, as well as guided the audience, or in our case the trainees, through the program simultaneously.

Keeping control also means that you have planned ahead for the use of your particular visual aid. If you are going to use a chart, make sure you have a place to set the chart that will allow it to remain in its full and upright position through your discussion. The last thing you want to be doing while discussing any audiovisual aid, such as a chart, is trying to hold it up so that it doesn't fall off the chalkboard or away from your training podium. You may have to even pay to have a trainee hold the chart if there is no other way to insure control.

Rule No. 4: Watch out for Murphy's Law. The most famous law, "If something can go wrong, it will" appears to apply most appropriately to audiovisual aids. How do you avoid this curse? Probably, you can't prepare for all of the eventualities. Traditionally, you will carry extension cords, extra light bulbs, additional magic markers, and chalk. Even that doesn't protect you from the evils that lurk in the training session. We recall once carrying an overhead projector, complete with the additional bulb, the long extension cord, and markers some two thousand miles to present a training program. We went down and looked at the room to make sure there were electrical outlets within distance of our extension cord and that the screen was there and that everyone could see it, in spite of several columns strategically placed throughout the room. Thus, we felt fairly confident that we had followed the general rule and would avoid the pitfalls of Murphy's Law. Needless to say, we were in for a big surprise when we set everything up, plugged in the overhead, and began the training program. At the point when we were to introduce the first overhead projection, we flipped the switch. Nothing happened. A quick check soon revealed that Murphy had struck again. Not only did the electrical outlet that we had used not work, but none of the electrical outlets in the entire room had power. Fortunately, we were not willing to let Murphy's Law overcome the situation, as we had prepared all of our overhead projections as handouts and were able to proceed without the use of the projector.

Perhaps the converse of this rule is most appropriate, and that is "Plan ahead and be prepared." Check out every conceivable pitfall that may befall you as you are using visual aids. If you have rehearsed your presentation with visual aids, try to do so in the room in which you will be providing training. Thus, you will be able to avoid Murphy striking you.

Specific Visual Aids

In our discussion of specific types of visual aids, we will look at each one of them from the point of view of how to use it, the optimum size of the audience for that visual aid, and the advantages and disadvantages of that visual aid. We will look at the aids by categories, beginning with written visual aids such as overhead projections, chalkboards, flip charts, and handouts. The second category will include audiovisual aids. The third category will include all other visual forms of aids such as films, slides, video, and computer-generated materials. We will conclude by talking about some of the nontraditional aids described in the beginning of the chapter.

Written Aids

When we think of traditional visual aids, we immediately think of using the chalkboard, flip chart, and overhead projector. For the most part, these types of visual aids simply highlight in writing those concepts that we are discussing orally. We use these aids to underscore our message, and to aid the trainee in remembering what we have talked about. They also serve the purpose of helping us maintain an outline and a flow for the material as we present it. In fact, some trainers have all of their notes in outline form on overhead projections and thus appear very organized because they can speak without having notes in hand or on the lectern.

The first, and often used, written a/v type is the chalkboard, or the modern variation, the wallboard, on which we can use erasable markers. Modern training facilities have gone with the latter approach as it is less messy and does not create the squeaking sound that chalk tends to as we write on the board. A chalkboard is most useful for highlighting particular words and a quick drawing of rather elementary graphs and tables. Its obvious advantage is that it is easy to use and can be done quite spontaneously. Unless you have a series of boards that can be hidden from view, however, you really cannot prepare materials on the chalkboard in advance of the training program. Chalkboards offer a limited amount of space on which to write, and can be messy. The optimum audience size could range from one to probably not more than twenty-five or thirty.

Like the chalkboard, the flip chart can be used for highlighting specific words or contents, as well as presenting graphs and simple tables. It, too, is easy to use, is relatively inexpensive, and the materials can be displayed in advance and revealed to the audience or trainees as needed. Pages also can be removed from the pad and attached to various walls around the training room for further use in the training session. On the other hand, the flip chart requires some kind of stand to hold it up and because of its size limits the size of the audience for its effectiveness. It probably is optimal between five and twenty to twenty-five trainees.

The overhead projector moves you into more advanced media, requiring both some kind of projection and a screen, or at least a wall, for the image. Like the chalkboard and flip chart, the overhead projector is useful for displaying key concepts, graphs, and tables. In addition, one can make overheads of anything that can be put through a copy machine. This means that even color photographs can be first copied on an overhead transparency and then projected to an audience. Thus, you have greater flexibility with the use of overhead materials.

On the positive side, materials for overhead projectors are relatively inexpensive and are fairly easy to prepare. One can also use the overhead in a spontaneous way simply by writing on clear transparencies in the same way that you would on a flip chart or on the chalkboard. On the other hand, effective use of the overhead projector requires advance preparation, as well as the purchase or rental of such equipment. The optimum size audience for an overhead ranges from five to approximately one hundred. If the audience approaches one hundred, you will find that a large screen, 25 x 25 feet, may be necessary and that you will be farther away from your overhead projector so that you will not have the flexibility of being able to write on the projector transparency and still be in front of the trainees. Thus, using an overhead for an audience of more than twenty-five or thirty can prove quite cumbersome and unwieldy. You will need an assistant just to change the overheads, because you will be far from the projector if you plan to stand in front of the trainees.

We should also talk about the latest variation on the traditional overhead. We now have the capability to generate overheads on a computer and display them on either an overhead projector or a television screen, depending upon the type of conversion device used. The equipment used to convert a computer-generated image for display on a television screen can be quite expensive. Regardless of the method used, remember the earlier rules regarding the ability of the audience to see and hear the material.

A piece of equipment out of the dark ages that has pretty well lost favor and should not be in your training repertoire is the opaque projector. This equipment is designed to project printed material from the page onto a screen. Given copy machines and the development of overhead transparencies, we seldom, if ever, see an opaque projector. The disadvantages far outweigh the advantages in that it requires a room with total darkness and a piece of equipment that is very large and cumbersome. The appropriate audience size would be much like the other three previously discussed.

The last form of written visual aid we discuss is handouts. There are several varieties of handouts that you can use with trainees, ranging from simple outlines to incomplete notes in which the trainee provides the additional information you discuss in the training program. Another type of handout is a collection of essays and/or articles. You would use these various types of handouts at different times during the training program. For example, it is best to present an outline before the training program so that the trainee knows where you are headed. If the handout is a series of incomplete notes, this might be appropriate for use during the training program so that the trainees can fill in the missing blanks. If you are handing out supplemental material or a series of essays, then it would be best to provide this after the training program. Remember, any handout material you provide the trainees can serve as a diversion from the training material you are discussing.

While the authors like handouts, we are well aware of the pitfalls of their use. We try to provide our handouts as needed, rather than providing the entire packet at the beginning of the training program. You can see the advantages and disadvantages of this approach. If you provide all of the materials at the beginning, you should be prepared for the trainees to wander through the training packet during the initial portion of your training program. If you provide each handout as needed rather than as a total packet, you need to find an orderly way to distribute the material. It can be very disruptive if frequently during the training program you have to pause to hand out the necessary material. This interrupts the flow of your training, can be disruptive, and can cause the effectiveness to diminish. On the other hand, we prefer handing out materials as needed so that we can use the material in any order that fits our needs at that point. It also allows for the flexibility to skip training handouts because the trainees already understand the concept. For example, if you have three different handouts on the use of interviewing techniques, you may need only one to get your point across. If you feel the others are valuable, you can always provide those at the end of the training program as supplemental material. On the other hand, if it is in a training packet that you have handed out in the beginning, you will feel obligated to go through all of the materials in the prescribed order; otherwise the trainees will be confused by going from page 1 to page 27, back to page 2, and so on.

We further feel that handouts are useful as an audiovisual technique because they help the trainee after the training session is over. We believe they serve as an aid to memory; as a trainee in one of our workshops put it, they became the bible for his training in presentation skills. In fact, after the pages became ragged, he called us for a new training program for his new employees because he felt the manual was a good tool that he could use almost on a daily basis.

There is really no limit to the number in your audience for the use of handouts. The only word of advice we would give is the larger the audience, the more it may be necessary to put your handouts into a packet to be given to trainees at the beginning of the session. One can really not take the time to wander among two hundred participants each and every time a new handout is needed. Therefore, you would provide the training packet at the beginning and would be expected to go through all of the material.

As you will learn in the next chapter, it is now possible to develop a series of overheads/slides using the computer. These slides can be printed one or more to a page as a series of handouts to reinforce the message.

Audio Materials

Cassettes, records, and discs can also serve the trainer in the presentation of materials. As with all a/v aids, their use depends on the type of material covered and the points that you are trying to make. We have found audiotapes to be quite useful as illustrations for a particular point, or to make examples to which trainees can respond. For example, if you were discussing the various types of empathic listening, you might put samples of dialogues on tape and ask the trainee to pick out which type of listening the person on the audiotape was doing. Audiotapes are relatively easy to produce, can be inexpensive, and are easy to use. With modern technology, audiotape recorders are fairly portable and with a microphone or an external speaker, can usually be heard by all members of the audience. On the other hand, overuse of audiotapes, because they lack the visual quality, can be somewhat boring to training participants.

There is really no limit on the size of your training audience for audiotapes and cassettes as long as everyone in the audience can hear them.

Visual Aids

In the category of audiovisual aids, we would include slides, films, videotapes, and computer graphics. These a/v types are the most stimulating for a training audience, but are the most difficult, time consuming, and expensive to use. Do not let that deter you from their use when it is appropriate for your training program.

The advantages of such visuals as slides, films, and videos are different for each, but the disadvantages are pretty much the same. The audience has to be of limited size, probably not more than twenty for videos, unless you have a number of monitors, and not more than one hundred for slides, or you will not be able to get a screen large enough to project an image that can be seen by everyone. The equipment is relatively expensive, but is rapidly becoming less expensive as new technology produces smaller and more compact units, particularly in the area of videotape.

Using professionally prepared slides, films, and videos can be quite expensive, because the supplier needs to build the cost of preparation and presentation into the actual expense of the film or videotape. For example, it can cost as much as $800 or $900 for a 20-minute film or video presentation. Prepared slide programs are also expensive, but are in the $100 to $300 range.

The advantage of using slides is that they are relatively inexpensive if you prepare your own, and are easy to use and quite portable. All of the advantages of the overhead projector can be duplicated by using slides, and you can develop sequence of items far more easily using slides than using an overhead projector. An additional benefit of using slides is that it is easy for you to develop vignettes or case studies for use by the training participants. In fact, you can develop a series of vignettes and ask the participants to follow through, expressing the outcomes of each of the scenarios you develop.

Films are advantageous because they allow you to present concepts in a process form where motion and a visual display are important. For example, you can have a film to demonstrate inappropriate leadership styles in management in an organization. The same can be said for the use of videotapes as can be said for films.

Many college and university facilities provide film and videotape libraries that are for rent at a nominal cost. If you have access to such materials, they can enhance your training program immensely. If you make your own videotapes, you will need to find some kind of a facility that will allow you lighting and limited editing equipment so that you can produce a video of quality equal to the rest of your training program. If your videos look homemade, you will create that impression with the trainees.

You might also consider videotaping portions of existing television programs to make your particular point. For example, when we are discussing the various forms of influence on individuals, we can use commercials prepared for the mass audience and discuss the various types of influence that are used by the advertiser. Vignettes from soap operas, evening television performances, and news programs can also be incorporated into videos to highlight points in your training program. Needless to say, all of this takes extra effort on your part in order to collect, edit, and use television as part of your video package. Note: Be cautious in using copies of television material because you do not want to violate copyright laws by copying and *distributing* these homemade collections.

Computer Graphics

While we will discuss the computer in more detail in the next chapter, we should point out that the computer offers a unique opportunity to generate graphics in the form of tables, graphs, and other charts that can be useful in combination with the more traditional forms of visual aids. Most software programs provide for the generation of computer graphics that can be used in training materials. The computer also offers the opportunity to generate free-form graphics through the use of an art board, which is available for most computers in the moderate to expensive price range. You should check with your local computer outlet to determine what is available for the kind of machine you have access to.

Computer Combinations

We have labeled this section a combination since the computer allows you to combine video, audio, pictures, and graphics into an output which then can be projected to a training audience via a conversion device. For example, you could develop a computer presentation that talks about different types of speech introductions by presenting first a word label followed by a brief audio/video within the computer presentation. The trainer could stop; ask questions; replay the video; and move on to the next segment. This same program could be developed into a self-taught computer package that a trainee could complete. Every day we get more and more sophisticated possibilities from computer applications. Check your favorite computer software store for the latest possibilities.

Nontraditional Aids

All of the audiovisual aids discussed so far are traditional in the world of training and development. There are a number of other items that you should also include in your repertoire of enhancements for training. You may be familiar with some of these, but we would certainly recommend that you look at them as viable options for your training presentation. These nontraditional aids include Play-doh modeling clay, Tinkertoy building blocks, pipe cleaners, puzzles, and magazine pictures. We would also include in this category all three-dimensional objects, which we might label as props. In addition to serving the usual role as a/v aids, these nontraditional forms can heighten the interest of your training audience. When conducting workshops on stress, we sometimes introduce Play-Doh modeling clay as a form of stress reduction. When we look at workshops on team building and small-group exercises, we use Tinkertoy building blocks as a basis for group activity. The same could be said for other props, as well as pipe cleaners and puzzles.

You should not overlook the use of pictures, ads, and other materials from the printed media, as they too can serve as a form of audiovisual aid. As we mentioned earlier, when we are talking about the role of influence in communication, we use television ads; the same could apply to magazine ads. When doing a workshop on creativity, the advertisement by the SAAB Motor Company as an illustration of right/left brain and the thinking process can be used. This is a good ad that caters to both the right and left brain (if you use and accept this approach) by providing a visual image for the right brain and a very analytical description of data about the car for the left brain.

The use of nontraditional forms of audiovisual aid is unlimited. Anything that can be used to demonstrate a point, add interest, or generate enthusiasm can be considered as a visual aid. Our only requirement is that the aid fit the particular point we are trying to make, rather than simply introducing it because it happens to be novel. We recall a speaker once who had a paper bag sitting on the podium through most of the presentation. At the appropriate moment, the person reached into the paper bag and pulled out several stuffed animals. He described the conformity of board members of the foundation like a row of ducks, saying yes when asked. Needless to say, the visual aid was well received and proved to be quite memorable.

Summary

In conclusion, then, there is a wide variety of audiovisual aids that can be used to enhance your training program. Let us underscore that whatever aid you select will work if it is appropriate for the material, as well as for the trainees to whom you will be presenting it. You cannot overprepare; i.e., making sure that all of the problems that can go wrong won't. Keep your aids simple, direct, to the point, and related to your discussion. Plan for failure. A wise person once advised that you should keep candles in your training packet, because when everything in terms of your visual aids goes well, there is always the chance that the lights will go out from a power failure. If this happens, relax, maintain your composure, and hope that the power will go back on quickly.

Using the Computer in Training

Objectives

This chapter will help you

► identify the uses for a computer in training
► recognize how a computer functions
► understand the hardware and software of computers
► recognize the interactive role of computers and video

Introduction

Whether we like it or not, computers touch the life of every person in a variety of ways. They keep track of our electric and gas bills, balance our checking accounts, keep track of our credit-card expenditures, control traffic, direct airlines, make theatre reservations, and arrange dates for us. For those of us interested in communication training, the computer is making inroads that offer both excitement and challenge. As we said in chapter 2, a trainer has to be able to cope with innovation and change. The computer is certainly creating both in training.

In the last chapter we talked about the computer as an aid for the presentation of information in training. In this chapter we will focus on the computer's role in the development of training materials and as a potential replacement for the trainer. If video was the innovation of training for the 1980s, the computer with video is the training innovation of the 1990s. We will discuss this role of the computer at the end of the chapter.

Before you panic at the thought of having to use a computer, we would like to arrest your fears. For most of the computer functions that we will consider in this chapter, you do not need to know how to program a computer. You will need to know how to use a microcomputer (one that fits on the top of a desk). If you know how to type and use a small calculator, you can use a micro. The mystique of the computer must be overcome since it will be an integral part of daily existence. You cannot shop at the supermarket or use an automatic teller machine (ATM) without coming in contact with a computer. In fact, most students in our elementary and secondary school systems have had the chance to become computer literate. We have done it, and we know you can too.

The best way to get to know about microcomputers is to browse the various computer stores in your location. Take demonstrations and read about the various functions and features of each of the computers. If you don't already own a computer, read the rest of this chapter and any of the popular books on the market that describe the uses and types of microcomputers currently available. Make sure that the computer you buy can do all that you want and still have the capability of growth for future uses.

We will not refer to specific brand names for computer programs (software) that are currently on the market because to do so would date the book. By the time this book goes into production, a whole new generation of software programs could be available.

Functions of the Computer

We would like to broaden your view of what computers can do for you as a trainer. Today's computers can do much more than analyze your data and keep recipes for future use. We will explore the five basic functions of the computer for training purposes: instructing, creating, accounting, analyzing, and communicating. How you use these functions will vary with your needs and your abilities. As we examine each of these functions, we will illustrate them with examples from various training segments in our field.

The computer's ability to store materials and analyze information frees the trainer for the important tasks of needs assessment and instructional design. To give you an example, both authors keep all of our training materials on computer disks so that we can use what may be appropriate for a given client. As we said earlier, we believe that each program should be designed specifically for the client. For example,we may keep a file on the barriers to communication in the computer. When we are going to talk about the barriers to communication for organization **XXX**, we just retrieve the communication barriers from computer storage and tailor them to the organization. When we work with organization **YYY**, we could apply the generic barriers to their situation.

Instructing

The disciplines of psychology and education have relied on the computer to assist learning. We can look at the two instructional applications of computer-assisted instruction (CAI) and computer-managed instruction (CMI). Computer-assisted instruction can involve direct instruction or can be used to assist the presentation of material by the trainer.

Direct instruction usually involves the presentation of material by the computer followed by questions that, if you get them right, allow you to proceed to the next section. If you select the wrong answer, you may be directed to review the material and to then make another selection. For example, let's assume that the material in this chapter was just presented by a computer and we want to know if you understand the concepts. The computer might now ask you:

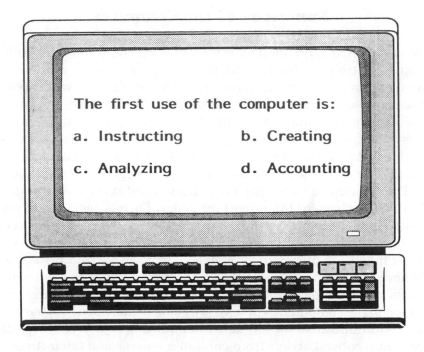

If you select d, the computer might respond: wrong, please reread the material. If you said a, it would proceed with more material or would present additional questions.

Such a process was called *programmed instruction* before we introduced the computer into the process. The same material, questions, and messages were provided in book form. You would read the material, answer a question, and turn the page to see if you had the right answer.

With computer graphics, we can enhance the messages we present to the trainee. In other words, we can use a visual aid within a visual aid (the computer). So we could use some computer-generated visuals to highlight key points for a topic we are teaching by computer.

One obvious advantage of CAI is that it allows the trainee to pace the instruction according to his or her own needs. If you have a number of computers or, conversely, a small number of trainees, you are free to help individual trainees as they progress through the program. Rather than lecturing, you are able to function as a true facilitator.

CAI also can be used after initial instruction as a form of repetition or drill. If you have conducted a session on the proper use of adverbs in written communication, you could save computer-generated messages that could check the trainee's understanding of the concept of adverbial use. Likewise, you can use CAI with the simulations, games, and other training activities discussed in chapter 7. You are only limited in your use of CAI by the availability of commercial programs or your ability to write computer programs on your own. We will discuss computer programming later in this chapter.

Computer-managed instruction has limited value to the communication trainer. Unless you are required to keep track of the progress of your trainees, you will not use the commercially available programs for CMI. Such programs keep track of trainees on a large number of exercises and give you a total performance score. This is useful if you have a large number of trainees and a number of training programs that can be taken in any order. For example, if you were running a training program for a company, you could track all of the employees who have gone through training, monitoring each trainee's progress. A print-out of your training log might look like the following:

	Training Topic			
	Listening	Group Process	Public Speaking	Total Score
Trainee 1	50	35		85
Trainee 2	35	30	25	90
Trainee 3		50		50

As you can see, only Trainee 2 has completed all three training units.

If you were required to test trainees on a given topic, CMI allows you to compile a test-item pool from which you could select questions for a given test. The computer will even select the questions if you tell it how many you need. Theoretically, you could have a different test for each trainee. CMI can be very useful for training programs that must test for certain proficiencies.

With CMI you are creating what the computer people call a *spreadsheet* (see above example discussing training topics). There are numerous such software programs available commercially for your use. We would caution you to find an integrated package of software that is compatible with others. For example, you would want software that allows you to move from spreadsheets to word processing and even to graphics programs without difficulty. Again, there are a variety of such packages on the market and we will not endorse one over the other. Why is integration important? The authors of this book are currently using two different packages of software, which means we must reenter (type) each other's material if we are going to make revisions via the computer. Needless to say, this is a time-consuming process and would be entirely unnecessary if we had used the same software package.

Another CMI tool is that of a computer *modem*. Essentially this is a device that allows you to communicate from your computer to another computer via a telephone hookup. This is important if you are working with a trainer in another city and want to share information quickly. For example, you could prepare your training materials and send them to your colleague for revisions via a modem. The revised material could be returned by modem to you in a relatively brief period.

The modem also allows you to retrieve data from the Internet, a system of linked computers from which you can retrieve information and materials from all over the world. For example, we wanted the phone number of a colleague at Ohio State University so we went through the Internet to a phone directory on the campus and retrieved the address, phone number, and some other demographic data about our colleague. At the risk of dating the book, we will talk more about the Internet later in this chapter.

The modem is central to your ability to communicate with the rest of the world so you should make certain that it is included with the computer you purchase, or that you can add it to whatever system you purchase.

CAI and CMI offer the trainer instructional opportunities to enhance learning for the trainee. It should be obvious that the computer cannot take the place of the trainer, at least not in its present form. Like audiovisual aids, which we discussed in the last chapter, the computer supplements your role as a trainer.

Creating

The most exciting prospects for the computer are yet to come. Considering the impact of the computer thus far has been limited to linear and numerical approaches, it is clear that by extending the range of the computer to three dimensional spaces, as we have seen with computer graphics, a visual revolution is at hand. With these graphics capabilities, you will be able to create exciting simulation and learning games for your trainees.

As we said in the beginning of this chapter, you do not need to know how to program a computer for most of what you can do in training. However, if you want to make maximum use of the creating function of your micro, you will need a working knowledge of a computer-programming language, unless your employer can provide a computer programmer for your unique uses.

Which languages you should learn and where you get the training are your choices. If you are still going to school, you might turn to the computer science department or business school for a basic computer-programming course. If you are out of school, you might look at community colleges for the same courses or explore what computer stores provide in the way of training. Another alternative is to use CAI and let the computer teach you how. Unfortunately, most computer manuals are not written with effective communication and clarity in mind. This approach may take you a little longer and be frustrating, but don't give up. It is well worth the effort.

Perhaps the most widely used creative function of the computer is word processing. This entire book was written using word-processing software. What is word processing? It is a glorified way of saying we sat down at a computer and typed the chapters. As stated earlier, we word processed all of our training materials and stored them on computer disks (think of disks as blank records on which you save information).

The big advantage of word processing and storage for the trainer is the ability to move, insert, and delete information in order to customize your training programs. For example, you may have to do a training program on presentation skills for a company. In storage (on a disk) you have materials on presentation skills that you used for a previous client. Using word processing you can transfer portions of that previous program into your new document without having to retype the entire package. Over a period of time you might have ten or more versions of a particular program that you can edit as needed.

Once you have the basic word-processing software, you can add a spelling dictionary, thesaurus, an outline function, and even check your grammar before you print a final copy. These features alone can save the trainer a lot of embarrassment with handouts. Remember, your credibility as a trainer is constantly on the line.

You can use word processing for a lot more than storing and editing training materials. If you need to develop questionnaires for needs assessment, the computer can facilitate it. You can put proposals to conduct training into storage as well. Once you have the material on a disk, you can save yourself time in drafting proposals and even final reports. For example, suppose you have submitted a proposal to do a needs assessment and training to the Triple Z Corporation. At the completion of training, the president of Triple Z would like you to submit a final report with recommendations for further follow-up. As you sit at your computer, you can have your original proposal on part of the screen (window), your training materials on another part of the screen, and can use the space remaining to write the final report. Any time you want material from your proposal or training documents, you insert into your final report those sections. Most software programs will allow you multiple windows to view several documents at once and patch back and forth. By analogy, you are painting a picture (final report) by combining what you see from several windows, all available at once.

An interesting series of software programs is emerging that enhances your creating capabilities. You are limited only by your imagination in drafting initial concepts or themes. If you have taken a small-group communication class, you probably had an opportunity to brainstorm. Now the computer can do a large part of that for you. The software brainstorms new combinations for the ideas that you developed originally. We do not want to focus on the types of software that can do this type of creating as they are changing on a daily basis. You need to examine what is currently available.

While the computer can aid you in the creating process, it cannot replace the creative act (so far, that is). If you cannot find the software you need to help you in the creative act, you may need to learn how to write (program) the necessary instructions so that the computer can help. Learning to program a computer is very useful to the trainer but it is the last step, not the first. If you know how to use software with your computer, you will be able to function fully as a trainer without programming skills. Adding those skills will take you one step beyond to make maximum use of your computer for creative training purposes.

Accounting

When we discussed the use of spreadsheets earlier in this chapter, we were talking about an accounting function of the computer. Trainers need to keep track of training materials, budgets, fees, schedules, clients, and appointments, to name a few. Effective use of the computer can organize these for you. Again, you will have to select the appropriate software programs or write them yourself. We recommend the former as it is easier.

For keeping track of schedules, appointments, and miscellaneous ideas, choose a type of software that is always at hand on the computer and can be turned to as needed. For example, if you are busy writing a training proposal and you get a call to set up a meeting, you can switch to your computer appointment calendar and schedule it. You can even make notes in your calendar for expenses, and so on. If you need a printed copy of your schedule, it is at your fingertips.

Whether you are working as a trainer in-house or as an outside consultant, you can use a spreadsheet to account for your various training programs. You can monitor all of the employees in the various stages of training, as we suggested earlier when we were discussing the computer-managed instruction function of the computer. You also can keep track of expenses, mileage, and other items required for tax purposes.

The beginning trainer will have less use for the accounting function of the computer, but if you start with such a program, you will be ready as the need arises. As we have stressed throughout this chapter, it is better to have too much capacity and software than to have too little and not be able to add because your computer does not have the capacity.

Analyzing

Another major function of your computer for training is that of analyzing. Essentially we are talking about the computer's ability to analyze data. For example, suppose that you gave all of the employees of your firm an attitude questionnaire about their views of the company. What do you do with the hundreds, perhaps thousands, of questionnaires that you collect? You could list each respondent's answers to the questions, or you could develop summaries of responses based on the averages of all the respondents. (If you are going to be using a computer to analyze data and do not have a basic knowledge of statistics, we suggest you review some elementary statistics reference materials.)

Entering all of your questionnaire data on the computer will allow you statistically to analyze your responses quickly and easily. Once the data are entered, the options for analysis are almost unlimited. You could find out what the majority of female employees thought about a particular issue, or what the employees who had worked for the company for more than ten years thought, compared to those who were new. Your only limits on analysis will be what you entered into the computer initially. If you did not ask the age of the employee, you could not use age as a basis for comparison.

Once you have analyzed the results and have a composite picture of employee attitudes, you could use a graphics software package to render striking visual images for the reader of your report. For example, if employees were asked how satisfied they were with the company, a graph of their responses might look like the pie chart in Exhibit 9.1.

Exhibit 9.1   Level of Employee Satisfaction

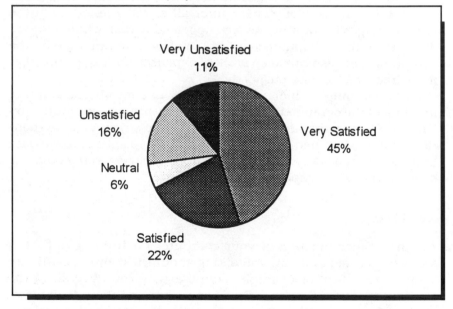

The uses of the computer for analysis are endless. As with all other functions of the computer, you are limited only by your knowledge of the computer's capabilities and your ability to use the software that is currently available.

Communicating

The newest and one of the most exciting uses of the computer is for communication. While members of universities have had limited ability to communicate with each other by computer, new technology has made such communication available to anyone with a computer, a modem, a phone line, and cash. You need the cash to connect to some system that will transmit your communication to others. The computer, modem, and phone line are your taxi or communication link to friends, colleagues, families, libraries, and data depositories around the world.

We will not discuss specific services currently offering this connection, only what you can accomplish generically. For example, your computer can serve as a fax machine. After generating a message or letter on your word processor, the computer can send it to a regular fax machine or to a computer which can read it as hard copy or as a file to be edited by the receiver using his or her own word processing. For example, the authors faxed chapters of this book back and forth to each other's computer. One could revise the other's material without making a paper copy. That same message may be sent by one of the Internet services, which would treat it as electronic mail. If you are sending your message as a fax, you need a phone line and a fax machine or computer at the other end. As an e-mail, you need a system that allows you to send or receive messages.

The computer as a tool for communication is still in its infancy. We would quickly outdate this book if we listed what is currently available—the technology for communicating via your computer will make great strides over the next several years. As trainers, we will be inhibited only by our ability to use the computer and our willingness to spend the money for the technology

Emerging Uses of the Computer

By now, we hope you realize the potential and the value of the computer for you as a trainer. We would like to conclude this chapter with a discussion of the computer as an integral part of a self-contained training program. By linking the computer with videotapes or videodiscs, you could prepare and deliver an entire training program. We began the chapter by talking about the computer as a teaching tool that both presented the material and tested users on their understanding of concepts. Combining the computer with video will allow you greater flexibility in the training function.

Visualize the following scenario. You want to teach a unit on leadership style in small groups to a number of new middle managers in your organization. You could develop a computer-training program that combines video examples (good and bad) of the various leadership styles. Each middle manager could go through the program at his or her own pace and not only learn the material but also practice the skills by identifying the leadership styles from video illustrations. Numerous examples could be called forth by the computer to meet the differing needs of the middle managers.

Using such a software program requires additional skills from a trainer. You must produce the videos as well as develop the computer-training package. There are software programs currently on the market that will direct you through the design and development process.

As with any training program, you must make certain that you are meeting the needs of the trainees and that the material you are delivering via the computer is as informative and interesting as it would be using the traditional formats of lecture, discussion, and case studies.

We could not end this chapter without speculating on the future of the computer in training. Although we now have computers that are voice actuated, they are not ready for mass production and widespread use in training. When that time comes, new training programs via the computer will emerge. In 1966, we suggested the day would come when a trainee could be videotaped making a presentation and the computer could be used to make an analysis of the message's effectiveness for a given audience. Using interactive video and computer programs, a trainee could present case studies orally and be given feedback by the computer, complete with an analysis of both the verbal and nonverbal dimensions of the presentation. Does this sound farfetched? It's not. That day has arrived and we, as trainers, have to be ready to implement it in our training programs.

Summary

We have selected to talk about general uses of the computer rather than list all of the hardware and software that is available. In the six years since the first edition of this book, one word-processing software has published six new versions. We would hope that the prospects of the computer would entice you to familiarize yourself with what is currently available.

The computer has progressed from a tool that can speed up complex, time-consuming tasks, to one that can make the editing and revision of text simple. It has advanced from accounting functions to diagnostic functions. For the trainer it has become the *one* piece of equipment that can make your work easier. It can never replace the trainer, but it can and will make you more effective.

Evaluating Training Programs

Objectives

This chapter will help you

► understand both the importance and the complexity of evaluating training programs

► identify various ways to evaluate programs

► recognize the strengths and weaknesses of evaluation methods

► identify ways to relate training to job performance

Introduction

One of the hardest things about training is evaluating it. How can you tell whether a program is effective or not? How do you measure its degree of effectiveness? What is the relationship between how much trainees liked a program and how much they learned from it?

Ironically, the degree of difficulty in evaluating programs is topped only by the political importance of the evaluation process. In many organizations, budget cuts often mean the training budget is the first to be pared down. This is an inappropriate decision in the long run, because it affects the organization's ability to perform well and grow. Many managers, however, feel short-term pressures more intensely than long-term needs. Without a clear idea of how training affects immediate performance in addition to long-range goals, managers easily dismiss its importance. Knowing this, the trainer must present results in terms managers understand. What specific effects did each training program have on *immediate* employee performance, as well as long-term performance, and how do these immediate effects translate to the bottom line?

Evaluating training is important, then, in at least two ways. First, it helps trainers learn what works and what does not. Through this information, trainers can improve the quality and effectiveness of their programs. Second, the evaluation process gives trainers a way to show management how the programs affect immediate as well as long-term needs. Because of the relatively weak political position of T & D, the trainer can benefit from using evaluation as a sales tool when dealing with other managers. The more clearly managers can see a relationship between how well trainees learned something and how much this learning improved current work performance, the more managers will support T & D.

The trainer must come up with evaluation procedures that are useful to him or her, to management, to teams, and to individual employees. There are several ways to evaluate training programs. The appropriateness of each method depends on various circumstances.

Trainees' Immediate Responses

Immediate responses from trainees come in two forms: the trainees' opinions of a program and the trainees' test results.

Trainees' Opinions

The most frequently used trainee response is opinion, usually in terms of how much a trainee liked a program. For example, a typical evaluation sheet asks questions such as these:

- What is your overall rating of this program?
  Excellent _____ Good _____ Average _____
  Fair _____ Poor _____

- How did the program match your expectations?
  Exceeded them _____ Met them _____
  Fell below them _____

- What is your overall rating of the trainer?
  Excellent _____ Good _____ Average _____
  Fair _____ Poor _____

- What is your rating of the audiovisual materials?
  Excellent _____ Good _____ Average _____
  Fair _____ Poor _____

- How well organized was the material presented?
  Very organized _____ Fairly organized _____
  Poorly organized _____

- How useful will this program be to you on the job?
  Very useful _____ Somewhat useful _____
  Not useful _____

While these evaluation questions may be reasonable enough, it is important to notice what they measure. They measure the trainee's opinion of the program—whether he or she liked the material, the trainer, the visual aids, and whether the trainee thinks the program will help him or her at work.

One weakness of these types of questions is that there is no clear relationship between liking and learning. Trainees may find a program humorous, entertaining, lively, and a good break from work, but may not necessarily learn anything that benefits them or the organization. As an example, one company offered two programs for secretaries: a how-to course in time management and telephone etiquette, and a motivational course designed to boost office morale. The programs were held in adjacent rooms.

Throughout the day, it was clear that the how-to course was, surprisingly, more entertaining than the motivational course, because trainees in the second program heard laughter all day from the room next door. The next day, however, it became clear that while the how-to program was fun, it did not teach much to the trainees; none of them remembered anything about time management or telephone etiquette skills. Enjoyment, then, is different from learning.

Another weakness of such questions is that trainees are not qualified to judge the relevance of material. Their input is important as a way of judging how well the trainer related the material to work situations. But trainees do not have as complete a picture of the organization, their departments, their teams, or even their jobs as do trainers and managers. The evaluation questions listed are useful ways to measure the trainees' perceptions of a program, but not to measure the program's effectiveness. In an engineering firm, for example, employees were asked to attend a program in interpersonal skills. None of the engineers who attended did so willingly; they did not see how interpersonal skills related to their drafting and designing work. From their managers' points of view, however, the engineers needed to develop these skills because the managers knew that due to changes in the company's marketing approach, many of the engineers eventually would be dealing more directly with clients. Because the managers had decided not to announce the changes until appropriate individuals were identified, the engineers were unaware of the need for the program, even though the managers knew it was relevant. Trainees, therefore, often are not able to judge the appropriateness of a training course.

While the trainees' opinions—the first type of immediate response—are important in terms of identifying trainees' preferences and perceptions, they are not meaningful ways to evaluate the effectiveness of a program. To judge effectiveness, trainees' test results—the second type of immediate response—are more useful.

Trainees' Test Results

A second type of immediate response from trainees is their scores on tests designed to measure how much they have learned. This response is more useful than opinion if the test does indeed measure what it claims to measure. As every student knows from classroom experience, doing well or poorly on a test does not necessarily reflect what is actually learned. Designing tests that accurately measure participants' learning is a difficult and challenging aspect of training.

One way to allow for legitimate testing is to clarify at the design phase of a program the objectives of the course. What will trainees know at the end of the program? If the trainer wants them to know the names and positions of engine parts, a clear way to measure this knowledge is to present, at the end of a program, a diagram of an engine and have trainees label the parts. If the objectives of a course include knowing company policy regarding confidential information, trainees can be asked, at the end of the course, to write down what the company's policy is. In both these cases, the trainer can tell whether objectives have been met by how accurately trainees answer these questions.

One weakness of this testing, however, is that open-ended questions such as "What is the company policy about confidential information?" lead to long essay-style answers that are both time consuming to evaluate and hard to standardize for comparisons. For these reasons, written tests often are in true-false or multiple-choice formats. In the case of company policy, sample questions might be:

- Confidential information is labeled with "XR."   T   F

- If a caller asks you for information that you think might be confidential, you should:
  (a) ask your boss what to say
  (b) refer the caller to the public relations department
  (c) give out the information
  (d) get the caller's phone number and give it to the information officer

These types of questions have weaknesses of their own. Multiple-choice and true-false questions often measure a trainee's ability to recognize rather than remember information. Fill-in questions provide a way to emphasize recall. A fill-in question might be:

- Confidential means the information is available only to _____ personnel.

As with essays, fill-in answers may be time consuming and may lead to decision making about answers that are only "close."

Another weakness in testing is that trainees may get good at test-taking, but not at applying the information to work. Every classroom has students who score well on tests but do not know how to use the information. Several ways to resolve this problem are discussed in the next section.

Another issue to consider in testing is whether trainees actually learned from the training program, or whether they may already have had the information. A way to determine this is to use the pretest-posttest method. At the beginning of the session, before any training starts, participants answer a pretest, that is, a test asking for knowledge about the information that is going to be covered. At the end of the training session, the trainees take a posttest—the same test that was used as the pretest. Ideally, the difference in scores would indicate how much the trainees learned. For example, if most of the trainees got 0 or 1 correct answers on a pretest of 25 questions and then got 24 or 25 correct on the posttest, these results would indicate that the trainees learned a great deal in the program. If they got 24 or 25 correct on the pretest, they obviously would not need the program. And if they got only 1 correct on the posttest, it would mean the program was not successful. A problem with this method, however, is that the very act of taking a test, as in the pretest, may tell trainees what to pay most attention to during the program. In addition, taking the same test twice—using "repeated measures," in research terminology—may improve trainees' scores simply on the basis of random chance. The pretest-posttest method has its limitations, although it can be very useful. Other testing methods are discussed in the section entitled "Types of Evaluation."

Trainees' immediate responses take two forms: opinions and test results. Their opinions are important in terms of telling trainers how receptive trainees are to existing and future programs. Test results, however, are more accurate measures of a training program's effectiveness. Accurate testing requires clear, specific objectives.

Relationship to Performance on the Job

Managers are eager to know whether training pays off on the job. As mentioned before, learning information does not necessarily translate into learning new behaviors. For example, in a workshop about performance appraisals, one manager consistently gave good answers when the trainer asked such questions as "What is the best way to use the appraisal as a form of motivation?" or "How do you help an employee feel comfortable about the appraisal?" Based on these answers, it would be easy to assume that this manager was proficient in giving performance appraisals. On the job, however, the employees in this manager's department were upset because of his blunt, negative comments. Clearly, the manager knew the right answers but was not able to use them. The same problem exists when a mechanic labels diagrams accurately on tests but cannot repair an engine on the job, or a receptionist correctly lists the five steps of telephone etiquette but speaks rudely and hangs up when callers irritate him or her. The information is of little value unless it improves behaviors on the job.

Types of Behaviors

Behavioral objectives must be set for programs designed to influence behaviors at work. Just as informational objectives state what a trainee should know at the end of the program, behavioral objectives state what the trainee should be able to do.

Sometimes these objectives can be measured immediately after the course. In a programming course, trainees are asked to design and run a certain type of program. In a hair-styling class, trainees demonstrate what they have learned by cutting and setting hair. These examples refer to specific skills that are relatively easy to observe and measure at the end of a training program.

Other behaviors require both time and the reactions of coworkers, employees, or bosses before they can be measured. For example, suppose managers took a course in ways to delegate. An informational test may measure how much the managers know, but only time and employees' reactions can tell how well they use what they know. In this case, the managers would practice the new delegation skills for a certain period of time—say, two months. During this time, employees would learn what effects the managers' delegation styles have on them. Do the managers select them for tasks on the basis of skills and interests, instead of favoritism or convenience? Do they give them enough authority along with responsibility? After this time period, employees would fill out—anonymously—a questionnaire asking such things as:

- Compared to six months ago, has your manager improved his or her delegation skills?

  Yes _____ No _____

- Does your manager make clear what you are expected to do?

  Yes _____ No _____

- Does your manager give you enough authority to carry out assigned responsibilities?

  Yes _____ No _____

Based on employees' responses, the trainer and the managers can determine the effectiveness of the program in behavioral terms.

This same process may be used at any level in organizations.

Several months after having employees attend a training course, bosses might fill out—anonymously—questionnaires about changes in employees' behaviors at work. If, for example, the training program dealt with time-management and organizational skills, the questions might include:

- Do your employees manage their time more effectively now than they did six months ago?

  Yes _____ No _____

- Does their work appear to be more organized?

  Yes _____ No _____

Sometimes, coworkers evaluate each other's work performance after a training program.

In all cases, the questions asked would be based on the behavioral objectives of the program: what trainees should be able to do on the job after the training. Whether the behaviors are immediately observable skills or longer-term behaviors within a broader context, they can be identified, asked about, and used at work.

The Bottom Line

Remember that the broad, long-term goal for all training is organizational productivity. In addition to specific job-related skills and behaviors, individual employee development, and improved departmental performance, training aims at increasing organizational effectiveness.

Effectiveness and productivity are difficult enough to measure. In most organizations, the bottom-line definition of these terms includes lower turnover, lower absenteeism, greater number of units produced, higher quality of production, increased sales, fewer accidents, lower costs, and increased profits. These outcomes are measurable in that they deal with numbers. What is hard, however, is determining how much these results are due to training and how much they are due to other circumstances, such as pay raises, the general economy, competition, new management, or other events. Even harder to measure, and harder to identify the source of, are such things as office morale, motivation level, dedication, support, and commitment.

Despite the difficulties in defining, measuring, and identifying causes for these outcomes, they are meaningful to organizations. Trainers must use cost-related measures when possible and, at least, behavioral objectives and outcomes to identify their contribution to the organization's bottom line.

Types of Evaluations

The pretest-posttest method was discussed briefly under the "Trainees' Test Results" section. While this probably is the most commonly used method in training, its weakness, again, is that there really is no way to determine whether increased knowledge indicated on the posttest is due to the training program or to other factors. Suppose a hotel holds a training program in housekeeping methods and several months later the rooms are noticeably cleaner. The posttest results—that is, the cleaner rooms—may be due to the program, but they also could be related to other circumstances, such as new vacuum cleaners, better-quality cleaning products, management's recent emphasis on improved room care, or any other possible causes. The pretest-posttest method does not say much about what caused the changes. To evaluate more accurately the effectiveness of training, several other testing methods are useful.

After-Only Design with a Control Group

Remember that the problem with the pretest-posttest method is that it does not clearly identify training as the reason for improved knowledge or performance. In the after-only design method, a control group is used to determine whether training made the difference.

In research, a control group is one that does not get the treatment you are measuring. In this case, the treatment would be the training program. The control group in an organization would be employees who did not get the training experienced by the treatment group, or the trainees. To keep everything else as equal as possible, the control group should be as similar as possible to the treatment group in terms of job titles, age, experience, gender mix, and other factors. Random assignment of employees to either the treatment or the control group ensures statistical equality between groups.

Using this method, no pretests would be given. The treatment group would go through the training program, while the control group would not. Both groups would take the posttest after the training was over. Suppose both groups scored about the same; this would mean the training had no effect, because the untrained group scored just as well (or just as poorly) as the trained group. In this case, training clearly made no difference. Suppose, however, the trained group scored much higher than the untrained group. Because the groups were equal in everything except the training, these results would indicate that training made the difference. Data analysis is used to determine whether the differences in scores are statistically significant or simply due to random chance.

There always is the chance—unlikely though it is—that the treatment group would score lower than the control group, meaning the training hurt trainees' skills! This is an example of a trainer's nightmare, and in the unlikely event that it occurs, the trainer's job is then to reexamine the program and the identified needs. Remember, everyone learns from mistakes.

Pretest-Posttest Design with a Control Group

In this method, employees again are randomly assigned to a treatment group or a control group. Here, both groups take a pretest, only the treatment group receives training, and both groups take a posttest.

Both groups are equal statistically, which means that differences in scores on the posttest can be attributed only to the training program, and not to group differences in intelligence, experience, or other factors. One advantage to this design is that the pretest results ensure equality between the groups. In case the results indicate inequality, statistical techniques may be used to correct the imbalance. Once again, statistical analysis determines whether differences in posttest results are significant—that is, whether they are due to the training program—or whether they are due to random chance.

Time-Series Design

While both methods just described use a single pretest or posttest, the time-series design uses a number of measures both before and after training. The purpose of this method is to establish individuals' patterns of behavior and then see whether a sudden leap in performance followed a training program. By having many data points to identify patterns, large variations legitimately can be attributed to the program.

One weakness with this method is that because of the relatively long time period covered, even large changes in behavior can be attributed to circumstances other than the program. For example, one company was eager to increase morale among employees in one department. Various training sessions were implemented, and because the topics included motivation and goal setting, top management expected that the sessions would increase morale.

Periodic testing indicated a sudden leap in morale, and management was tempted to interpret the leap to mean the sessions were successful. The leap, however, coincided with replacement of the department's manager. Obviously, the increase in morale could be attributed to more than one event. Here again, use of a control group can make a difference. All employees would have gone through similar circumstances, such as changes in management, raises, job pressures, or other events.

Solomon Four-Group

This method uses more than one control group, and its purpose is to minimize the effect that pretesting may have on trainees. Because of the possibility that the act of taking a pretest changes trainees' attitudes toward the program, this complex design attempts to account for these effects.

In this method, trainees are randomly assigned to one of four groups. Group 1 is a treatment group—that is, a group receiving the training—that takes a pretest and a posttest. Group 2 is a control group that takes the pretest and posttest but takes no training. Group 3 is a treatment group that gets training and takes only the posttest, and Group 4 is a control group that does nothing but take the posttest (see Exhibit 10.1).

With this design, neither control group has received the training and only one has taken the pretest. Through statistical analysis, the trainer can determine what differences both the training and the pretest made. One major limitation with this method is that it is not really practical in ongoing organizations. Nevertheless, it is used in research projects when the situation allows for it.

Multiple-Baseline Design

Another complex method is the multiple-baseline design. This method compares the performances of individuals within groups, rather than between groups. In this case, the multiple baselines are the individuals' current levels of performance. Differences—and, it is hoped, improvements—in each person's level of performance are compared to the original baselines. The individuals are controls for themselves.

The trainer who uses this method is trying to determine whether improvements occur only after training programs, or in some other random fashion. Suppose the baselines of individual salesclerks showed certain levels of performance in terms of accuracy and

Exhibit 10.1   Solomon Four-Group

Group	Pretest	Training	Posttest
One	X	X	X
Two	X		X
Three		X	X
Four			X

speed on the computerized register, and suppose the clerks take a training program in using the register, after which their speed and accuracy increase. If this procedure were repeated over time, and the pattern showed that performance increased after training, and only after training, the results would indicate that training made a difference.

All these methods provide various ways to evaluate the effectiveness of training programs and to determine that it truly was training that made the difference. Because of their need to "prove" its worth in terms of the bottom line, trainers must consider the evaluation aspect even when designing programs. It would be to the trainer's advantage to keep management posted regularly about evaluation results.

Long-Term Implications

A combination of things makes evaluation a key element of training. As mentioned earlier, management must see the direct relationship among training, behaviors, performance, and the bottom line. The trainer truly must sell this relationship to management. Computer technology allows for sophisticated and usable statistical analysis to serve as a tool for the trainer. Because the evaluation procedure is crucial both in terms of its implications about training programs and its political uses, the trainer must identify the appropriate evaluation method while designing the program.

Despite the emphasis on the need to use statistics in the evaluation process, a word of caution is in order. Sometimes, the computer and statistical processes can seduce a trainer into a "research for research's sake" approach. Remember that the purpose of training is practical—that is, the results must be relevant and useful to the organization and to society. Research is valuable, but only if it is applicable to the needs of the trainees and the organization.

Summary

The evaluation process is both a difficult and crucial part of training. Programs can be evaluated in a number of ways. One category of evaluation methods involves trainees' immediate responses. These methods include trainees' opinions and trainees' test results. Another category of methods attempts to measure the relationship of training to performance on the job. These methods are concerned with types of behaviors and the bottom line.

Types of evaluations include pretest-posttest, after-only design with a control group, pretest-posttest design with a control group, time-series design, the Solomon four-group, and multiple-baseline design.

Because training departments are politically weak in most organizations, trainers can use the evaluation process to show managers the contributions training makes to the organization. The trainer may use statistical methods to strengthen his or her position, but must remember that the bottom line always must be practical and usable.

The Ethics of Training

Objectives

This chapter will help you

► understand ethics in training

► identify when to recommend training

► understand the confidentiality of individual employees when conducting assessments

► recognize responsibilities regarding plagiarism and copyright with training materials

Introduction

Ethics on the job may be a hot *training* topic, but we are convinced that it should also be a hot *trainer* topic. In this chapter we would like to talk about what we consider to be the role of ethics from a trainer perspective, rather than as a topic for training.

Common Ethical Concerns

Perhaps the biggest ethical dilemma we face as trainers is the decision to make recommendations that might not call for training. If our job description says that we should do training, then we are caught in an ethical dilemma if, in fact, training might not be called for. We would be no better than the physician who makes an inaccurate diagnosis calling for surgery and then performs it.

Suppose we determine that an organization has a problem of leadership in management positions. Should we recommend that we train the managers or tell the CEO that two managers were identified as ineffectual? We suggest that you spell out the alternatives to the CEO, and let that person make the decision. A few years ago, we identified a specific manager who was ineffective. The CEO valued that employee and chose to have all managers go through a training program rather than fire the ineffective individual. We gave the client the options and let him (in this case) make the decision. This, then, is one of the biggest dilemmas we have to face as trainers.

A corollary dilemma is making a nontraining recommendation beyond our expertise. In the above example did we have the expertise to tell the CEO to fire the two managers? Probably not; that should be his or her decision. We have the expertise to make a judgment as to whether someone is an effective communicator or manager and nothing more. In one assessment that we did a few years ago, we determined that the top three levels of management were ineffective. We did not recommend termination but made our recommendations for training and organizational change. As it turned out, the Board of Directors ultimately chose to terminate all of them rather than reorganize or train. We may have agreed but it was beyond our expertise to tell them to terminate.

We are of a mind that we have an obligation to report *what is* and hope that there will be enough opportunities for us to do training or, if not, to expand our job so that it incorporates more than the training function that we've described throughout the book. We make our livings conducting training for a variety of clients, so we walk a fine line when we make an assessment for an organization, and then propose that we conduct the training. We are telling them what is wrong and that we can fix it with training.

A second ethical concern emerged previously when we talked about doing a needs assessment and reporting that assessment in written or oral form. The ethical issue comes up as we try to balance the presentation of information and the maintenance of confidentiality. Not asking for names or other identifying information may not ensure confidentiality. One of our students, when doing a needs assessment, reported that the supervisor stood over each employee while the questionnaire was being completed and then collected each one. Confidential? Probably not! Did the student get accurate information? No. Interviews with employees indicated they were afraid to give an accurate picture of the company for fear the supervisor would see their comments. We must protect individuals when they respond to us. We are convinced that confidentiality must be maintained or our integrity as trainers and human resource people will be seriously jeopardized. We have an obligation, on the one hand, to report as fully as we can on the issues and concerns that emerge. We have the further obligation, however, of presenting the report in such a way that information can be brought to light without exposing specific individuals to whom we have promised anonymity.

We recommend that you not report data if it will isolate a small number of persons within the organization. For example, if a department has nine females and only one male, you should not report gender differences. Examine each comparison point to see if it will isolate and thus identify individuals. If it does, you are violating confidentiality.

A third ethical dilemma can arise when doing a needs assessment for a CEO or other top management person. Suppose a CEO hired you to find out why production was off and turnover was high. Your needs assessment turned up reasons which, "when corrected," would aid management but might hinder the employee. What should you do? Should you go ahead and make the recommendation to the detriment of the employees? You should know up front what implications there may be from an assessment. Are you willing to make a report that will cost employees their jobs? Are you willing to tell the CEO that she or he is the problem? Your obligation is to complete an accurate assessment regardless of the outcome. If you cannot do so, you are better off not accepting the assignment. No textbook can provide all the answers for you, but we hope you will deal with these questions when appropriate.

We have resolved these questions for ourselves by being very selective about our clients. We attempt to learn as much as we can about the corporate philosophy before we agree to a project. We have that opportunity because we have been working in training for a number of years. For those who might now be wondering: yes, we have said no to clients because of issues regarding management philosophy.

Training Materials

While we personally have never been concerned that others use training materials that we develop and present, we would certainly feel that, as trainers, we have an ethical obligation to point out when we are using materials developed by other people, and would encourage full compliance with copyright and use procedures on all instruments designed for needs assessment or training. We've seen numerous examples of tests that are so similar to something that has been copyrighted by someone else with no credit given to the original source. That's not to say that there are not materials out there that have been used in so many different ways that the original source may be totally obscure or forgotten. On the other hand, when the source is known, it's our responsibility to credit that source or even seek permission if we are going to use the materials on a wholesale basis.

This problem extends to the use of computer software that is used in the development of the training materials. There are copyright laws concerning computer software that we recommend you read and follow. If you don't have the manual for the software you may already be in conflict.

Professionalism

Finally, we have a moral, if not ethical, obligation to do our very best as trainers. There is no question that, historically, many training departments have served as dumping grounds for employees who really did not fit in or could not carry out their responsibilities in other departments. Putting such a person in training was a way of getting that individual out of the mainstream and out of the way of producing units within the organization. But training is too valuable to relegate to this kind of an individual, and we believe we have a moral obligation to make sure that we do our best to maintain the integrity of the training and development profession.

You have an obligation morally if not ethically to keep up to date. You should strive to keep current in your area of expertise. If you have been in a classroom where the instructor used the same old yellowed and tattered notes to lecture, you know what we mean. Clearly some training areas change more rapidly than others.

We have tried not to be too prescriptive in establishing a code for trainers, but that may be where the field is headed. In a survey conducted by the Center for Business Ethics at Bentley College in Waltham, Massachusetts, 208 of the top 1000 companies within the United States reported having written codes of ethics, and 99 have formal training programs in the area of ethics. It is a growing concern and one in which we, as trainers, should be proactive rather than reactive. If we establish our ethical standards up front, there will be no need to come back and respond at a later date.

As we have, you must develop a personal code that you will follow as you move into the training field. Here are some guides that we follow as we perform assessments and training:

1. We will not conduct assessments unless we have the cooperation of top management.
2. We will not conduct training without the enthusiastic support of top management.
3. We will not conduct training without the opportunity to observe and/or interview prospective trainees.
4. We will not deliver a "canned" program for training.
5. We will work with companies that have a positive regard for their employees.
6. We will not cancel a training program because a better contract comes along.

Our intent is not to get you to follow our code but to recognize the need for a set of principles that you can follow comfortably. Following your own guidelines will help you avoid inconsistencies that could result in the loss of business, or even your job if you work in-house. Are our guidelines right for everyone? Not necessarily, but they work for us.

Summary

As a trainer you have to be prepared to deal with ethical issues on several levels, including making nontraining recommendations, maintaining confidentiality, and determining when the implications (e.g., lost jobs) of doing an accurate needs assessment might preclude you from accepting the assignment. Moreover, trainers must exercise caution and good judgement when using training materials developed by others, particularly with regard to copyright infringement. Finally, trainers have a moral obligation to serve clients to the very best of their ability. This means keeping up-to-date on developments in the field as well as establishing a personal code of conduct. By adhering to such principles, trainers help maintain the integrity of the training and development profession.

Future of Training and Development

Objectives

This chapter will help you

► identify directions for the training field

► recognize the foundations of training and development

► identify training topics for the future

► understand the steps for entry into training and development

Introduction

No other aspect of communication has a greater potential than training and development. The future for training is bright, not only because of the demand for people who have training skills, but because training offers a combination of research and teaching skills in an ever-changing environment.

As we suggested, there is a greater need now for trainers than ever before. This is primarily due to three major changes in the way society functions. First, society itself is undergoing very rapid change in the ways we accomplish things; the ways we now process ideas; and the ways we conduct ourselves in our jobs. This rapidly changing society demands that we constantly upgrade our skills so that we can adjust to the needs of our jobs and our environments. For example, many of you, just like the authors, have had to go from typewriter to computer in order to do what we now label *word processing*.

The second major reason the future looks so bright is that we have reached what many of the futurists call the *information age*. As a result, we process information rather than material kinds of things on some form of an assembly line. We will talk more about this a little later in the chapter, but we would like to give you an overview now.

The third reason is that corporations are increasingly interested in continuous, "just-in-time" learning. They want more immediate problem-solving experiences in "real-time"—that is, more help solving the actual problems they face. A skilled trainer/facilitator will continue to be in demand.

Certainly we are not writing the book to speculate on the future of training and development, but would like to look at essentially four areas to help you prepare yourself for what tomorrow has in store. First we will look at the underlying foundations of the training field as we move toward the year 2000. Next we will prognosticate a little bit and look at the topics and processes for training that we think trainers will be involved with for the rest of this century and into the twenty-first century. Finally, we will consider the ways you can get into training should that not be what you are now doing.

Foundations

In case you haven't noticed, society has changed to the point where we have more people now employed in service industries than we do in manufacturing and related fields. Certainly, training is a service, even though it is conducted on a very professional level. People are moving to service-related jobs because production has been mechanized to the point that assembly-line skills and other basic jobs are no longer necessary. Witness the demise of industries like the copper industry, as an example.

What does that mean for us? As more people move into service-based industries, the more they are going to need what we would call *people skills*. Service is essentially offering something to another individual. Therefore, when we offer household cleaning or maid service, we are attempting to communicate our ability and credibility to the person who might hire us. Therefore, service industries are very people oriented. With this people orientation, those who go into the service industry must recognize that the skills they need are very much oriented to selling and motivating people.

As trainers we have the opportunity to develop these skills in people who go into the wide variety of service industries. We are convinced that training has a lot to offer such people, particularly in the field of communication. What better skill to develop in a service-type employee than the ability to communicate and to sell the services that he or she has to offer? That's our job as trainers and something we can look forward to as we move into the twenty-first century.

What caused this movement to service-related training was a mass shift in the development of manufacturing and assembly-related skills. Through the 1940s and 1950s, most training centered on the development of the mechanical skills necessary for assembly-line work. With the shift to less manufacturing and assembly work due to automation, industries no longer need a trainer who can provide this very technical expertise. As we suggested earlier, the trainer of today is one who can help people relate to other people as they provide the services or the management skills for the very few who might still be in some kind of manufacturing role.

A second major foundation in the future of training and development is emerging from what we would call a *communication/transportation society*, rather than the industrial society of the past. This is not a new concept; other futurists have written about it for many years. In essence, these writers are suggesting (as we are) that society is at a point where it relies less on transportation and more on communication. From our discussion in the chapter on computers, you should already be aware of the amount of communication that takes place between individuals via the computer network. With the telephone video, and the computer, we will rely less on transportation in order to get messages around.

We now communicate with our colleagues around the world via electronic mail. We type a message to a friend in Berlin and get a reply via computer almost immediately.

A greater emphasis on communication will create a demand for trainers who can provide the skills necessary to communicate effectively. As we suggested in the chapter on computers, any understanding of communication must be assisted by knowledge of the microcomputer. We believe these two skills go hand in hand. Communication is the outcome, the computer provides the means for that communication to occur. You will still need to understand and to train in interpersonal communication skills, but you may be operating with a personal computer rather than in a face-to-face setting.

A third major foundation for the future, again, has been hinted at throughout this book. As Toffler and others like Naisbitt have suggested, we are in an information age. We are being bombarded by information and must learn how to cope with the volume of material we receive in both written and oral form. As a trainer in the field of communication, this development can only be exciting, and serve as a challenge as one develops the necessary skills. As organizations become increasingly demanding about just-in-time learning, they need trainers who can help them improve the *process* of learning, as well as the learning of specific topics.

As early as 1983, Williams and Dordick posited five changes that would affect us in this information age. First, communication, as we suggested earlier, is becoming a substitute for expensive transportation. Look at the success of the Internet. Second, information increasingly is becoming a commodity in our post-industrial economies. Third, network information services are bringing everything from banking to shoe shopping into the home. Fourth, electronic leisure is one of the fast-growing components of our society—including television, pay TV, discs, video games, home computers and so on. Finally, the most exciting uses of technology for educational purposes are occurring more rapidly in business than in our public schools or universities. As a trainer you may find state-of-the-art facilities in which to work with your trainees. Keep in mind that to be effective, you must keep up with the latest changes in this information age.

If it is industry and business that will make the true advances in education and training, the impact in these areas will be felt in the home as more and more households have their own personal computers, as well as video recording and playback equipment. You only have to go to the local video store to see the number of self-help tapes, CDs, and training programs that are already provided.

These training programs go beyond simple golf lessons and aerobics. You can go to the computer store and see the same development in discs and cd roms.

All of these issues we have talked about so far provide the foundation for a very exciting future for the individual in training and development. Regardless of the state of the economy, there will be a need for people who can train other people to communicate and to survive in an information-based society. The person who is knowledgeable about people skills and who has the ability to apply those people skills to technology will certainly have the edge in the years to come. With this foundation, you should then prepare yourself to develop skills in certain topic areas.

In the next section of this chapter, we will discuss some of the key areas, particularly in communication, we feel have a potential for significant training and development programs. As we said in the beginning of the chapter, it is difficult to speculate on what will happen one year into the future, let alone five years. We think that our prognosis is good, since it is based on our study of the training and development field, as well as on an examination of what other futurists have had to say. As far as topics are concerned, we see seven key areas in the field of communication that we think trainers should focus on in the short and long term.

Topics

First and foremost, the trainer should develop skills to assist trainees in enhancing their abilities to cope with change. Trainers should be asking questions like "How do we communicate change?" "How do we adapt to change using communication as the underlying process?" These questions are among the most important ones that trainees will have to face in the years to come. We know how our knowledge base has rapidly increased in geometric proportions; that will only continue. If knowledge has doubled in the past few years, just think of how much faster that knowledge base will double in the next few years.

A second area of communication important for future trainers is listening skills: those that make us both critical listeners and empathic listeners. It is not our intent to go into a full discussion of these topics, as you can do additional reading should they pique your interest. Listening is emerging as a critical topic in business and in the short term this should grow even more rapidly. In the long term, we will see listening being integrated much more with the other half of the communication process, namely that of communicating.

The third area of focus for trainers is public speaking. Perhaps no other skill has been demonstrated to separate the true leaders from followers as has public speaking. We will continue to need an emphasis on public speaking as part of an effective training program. Certainly, as a part of this emphasis, we will need to develop videotape feedback as part of the training process.

The fourth communication skill needed for training is the ability to facilitate groups, as well as to develop good group communication skills. We are seeing the need to develop individuals who can help groups solve problems and negotiate. The kind of training we are talking about here is not necessarily that of developing group leaders, but preparing individuals to go into a group they may not be a part of, and facilitate or negotiate that group toward the resolution of problems and/or conflict. It is these facilitation and negotiation skills that are becoming more important.

As a corollary of the facilitator and negotiator skills, trainers need to develop within trainees the ability to use the group process for problem solving. In the past, we may have encouraged the use of traditional problem-solving methods, however, such procedures as brainstorming and nominal group technique are just as important.

Next, as a logical adjunct to the development of group process, we are seeing a continued interest in the area of conflict and conflict resolution. This is certainly a skill that communication trainers can provide, even to the point of training in the area of negotiation. Business is finding a great need for people with negotiation skills to facilitate contracts and business's relationship with public and other civic-minded groups. For example, industries increasingly find it necessary to negotiate with environmental groups over issues of plant operation and pollution. As trainers, we can train people in the art and science of conflict negotiation and resolution.

As interpersonal communication comes to the forefront, one particular area we had hoped would dissipate has only increased. That area is one that we're seeing a great deal of press about: stress and stress management. While this may be viewed as a topic for someone whose interest is psychology or psychiatry, communication plays a very big role in stress management and reduction. As trainers, we should offer our skills in interpersonal communication toward the resolution of stress that might be brought about not only by the work environment but also by a trainee's interpersonal relationships with others. This can be a big source of stress and one that communication can certainly help resolve.

Last, and certainly not least, we are seeing a resurgence in the understanding of ethics, particularly as it applies to business. While we are not in the business of teaching ethics per se, communication trainers can certainly offer training in how to communicate about ethics. This topic is beginning to come back into vogue in business. We can offer our facilitation skills to help business, industry, and government resolve some of the significant issues in the fields of situational and related forms of ethics. This topic, as can be seen in recent business publications, will only continue to grow in importance.

These are the key areas we feel will continue to develop and emerge as communication-based topics for training in the decades to come. We would add one area which combines all of the above topics under one label—customer service.

We believe that the information age combined with the increased emphasis on service industries will demand that employees learn how to deal with customers, consumers, and the receivers of products. It will require a trainer who is skilled in the above communication topics and also knows about technology.

Processes

Having discussed the skills that effective trainers will need to possess, we now want to look at how our training roles will develop as we try to train those around us.

If the media and the computer become the basis for information exchange, the role of the trainer will change drastically in the future. Where training in the past may simply have involved the processing of information, the trainer of the future will have to play a far more dynamic role. Two computers can exchange information, but it is the human and computer in the exchange process that will require the ability of the trainer. Trainers will take on the very important role of interpreter and maybe even that of mediator to ensure that the parties to the communication via the computer understand their complex roles as they interact. It will be the trainer's task to make sure that we understand and are understood in our communication with others. Technology can aid in the transmission of this information, but training will be needed to explicate the nuances of the meanings to the messages. Thus, even if technology grows rapidly, we will still need the trainer as a facilitator between the person and the machine.

We fully expect, then, computer-assisted instruction in educational technology to be a central force in the training process. We will see computers used not only alone, but also with videotape as a means of providing training on a wide variety of topics, including communication.

Another area where processing communication is concerned is that of teleconferencing. A good trainer is going to have to know how to reach groups in a wide variety of settings, since we have already suggested that communication will take the place of transportation. For example, one state bar association provides continuing education training for its attorneys through teleconferencing, rather than putting on a conference in a major city and expecting all of the attorneys to show up at that site. Thus, a speaker can be training live in one facility and via teleconferencing network can be sent to fifteen or twenty other locations throughout the state at much less expense than bringing all the attorneys into one environment. Multinational and national companies will see this as a way of providing training for a large number of employees at a much reduced cost. Your role as trainer will be to facilitate such teleconferencing training efforts.

Last, there will continue to be a need for what we have called the stand-up trainer. Not every organization will be able to afford television, computers, or teleconferencing, but they will be able to afford an individual who will provide the training. This role will continue, but for you truly to get ahead in the training field you are going to have to know how to adapt to all of the other processes for training that we have described.

As we said earlier in this chapter, self-help audiotapes and videotapes and computer variations of discs and CDs are on the increase. As a means of providing training, this process will only continue to grow. Our goal as trainers will be to provide viable learning experiences by such self-help tapes, either through the companies we work for or through some sort of free-lance effort. This is big business and should be part of our training repertoire.

Most of the processes we have talked about in this chapter relate to your role as a trainer working for some organization, rather than working on your own. We would suggest that you read the appendix to this book if you are approaching the field from a self-employed point of view. If you are thinking of being a full-time, free-lance trainer, there are many other issues that you will have to face in addition to the topics and the processes that we have described.

Needless to say, whether you are approaching training from within an organization or as a free-lance consultant, you will have to know how to market and advertise your training programs. We say marketing and advertising from *within* and outside the organization because we believe that the trainer must take an active role in developing a market for training programs. We are suggesting that the effective trainer of tomorrow is one who is proactive rather than reactive. You should not sit back in your training department and wait for some manager or CEO to come to you and say, "We've got a problem. We need training in participative management." The viable training organization is the one that is constantly out talking with employees and with managers to find out what the needs are and what should be made available in the area of training. This is true for the in-house trainer as well as the free-lance consultant. It is the proactive trainer who will make a mark and have a future in the training field.

Entry

The last topic we would like to consider in terms of your training future is how one can get into the field of training. Essentially, there are four ways that most trainers get into the field. We would like to look briefly at each one of these.

First, there are educational programs that are designed for someone who wants to go into the training and development field. These will vary from one or two courses on the topic to entire degree-related programs combining marketing, advertising, communication, small business practices, and other related skills. We would encourage you to look at various degree catalogs to find out what programs are available to pursue academic credentials in the training field. Moreover, many universities are designed to accommodate the schedules of working adults.

As a corollary, there are a number of professional organizations that offer workshops that vary from one day to three weeks on how to be a consultant. It is not our intent to evaluate these programs, but to suggest that they, too, offer an option for someone who wants to get some kind of educational background in the field of training and development, but who does not have the time to pursue a four-year degree program at a college or university.

Second, if you are already employed in an organization, you can attempt to transfer to the training department, if one exists in your company. If such a department does not exist, you can, as a number of our students have done, offer to work in the training area until a department has been developed, with the hope that the student might then become the training and development person. It is not always easy to transfer into the training department unless you have taken the time to develop your educational background through a degree program or through the seminar approach to build your credentials in the training area.

An alternative way to build your credentials for a possible transfer within the organization is to volunteer to do training programs for your company. By demonstrating that you have the skill and that what you have to offer is valuable, you may be able to persuade management that you belong within the training area. One of our former students reported that she constantly volunteered to conduct training in addition to performing her entry-level job. After a year of successful training experiences using this volunteer approach, she was transferred to the training department. Had she not volunteered, she would still be at the entry level. You cannot always wait for opportunities; you must make them.

The third way you can break into training is simply to strike out on your own. If you read the appendix carefully, you will see that we do not suggest this alternative unless you have built up a good cash reserve and are prepared for a bleak period until you develop your clientele. To strike out on your own, you also need credibility, experience, and expertise in a topic area that is viable in the training field. If you have these, as well as some good marketing skills, there might be an opportunity for you to go out on your own and be successful.

The fourth and final suggestion for breaking into the training field is through an internship program. You can go to a university or college and check with the appropriate department to see if they have a formal internship program. If they do, you can sign up for that program and receive credit. Essentially, what you are doing is working for an organization much like an apprentice did in years past, without pay in most cases, but with the opportunity to gain credit and experience.

This may not be an alternative if you are already employed on a full-time basis, and therefore cannot quit your job in order to do an internship. What we would suggest here is that if you are really interested in breaking into training, you ought to volunteer to do an internship, either with your organization or with an organization that you would ultimately like to be a part of. This may mean evenings, weekends, or adjusting your work schedule in order to accommodate an internship.

Our experience over the past eight years in running internship programs convinces us that whether it is paid or unpaid, whether you receive academic credit or not, the internship proves to be one of the most valuable experiences one can gain in any field, and we would say in training specifically. You have an opportunity to learn on the job without risk of making a shift until you are truly convinced that's the area you would like to be in. An internship or on-the-job experience will prove invaluable; we cannot impress upon you enough the importance of an internship or apprenticeship. If you look at the want ads, you will recognize, as we have, that most training positions want candidates who have had experience. If you are just out of school or just switched careers, you may be long on desire, skills, and motivation, but short on experience. An internship in whatever form can give you valuable experience.

Summary

In this chapter we have discussed the foundations for training and development in the decades ahead. We believe there are several key issues to keep in mind, such as a service-based society, less emphasis on manufacturing, and more emphasis on communication and information. With that basis, the need for trainers will grow rather than diminish. We have also looked at what we consider to be the viable content areas for training in the decades ahead and the processes by which we will train in the future. Finally, we have offered four suggestions as to how you can break into the training field, recognizing as you do now that it's an exciting, rewarding field to be in. You need to build the training program and your role in it by getting actively involved as a volunteer or intern. You have to build your credibility as a trainer.

Appendix:
Setting Up a Consulting Business

Objectives

This appendix will help you

► identify the requirements for setting up a consulting practice

► understand the pitfalls of setting up a business

► recognize the minimum requirements for a consulting business

► identify the basics of private consulting

You have made it through the entire book and you are still excited about the prospects for the field of training and development. You've considered all of the options and decided that you really don't want to work for someone else; you would like to be in business for yourself. We can only warn you that the road to financial independence in your own consulting business is a long and arduous one. We have tried over the years to encourage our students to seek a corporate position but there are still a few who go into consulting and prove us wrong. Rather than dissuade you further from this goal, we would like to talk about what you can do in order to be successful as an independent consultant.

Where Do You Start?

Before you buy your business cards and hang out your shingle as a private consultant, you need to sit back and decide exactly what it is that you're going to offer the world as an independent consultant. If you don't have a Ph.D. and five or more years of experience in the training field, you should probably start with a look at your own personal development. Namely, you should develop a list of personal strengths, followed by a description of the skills you could offer others through a series of workshops or training programs. What you are going to have to do is create two lists, one of your strengths in order to determine whether or not you could really make it as a consultant, and one of skills you feel others would be willing to pay for in order for you to have a successful consulting business. Let's look at the personal strengths first.

As we indicated in the first two chapters of this book, you need to have a strong self-concept as an initial starting point, whether you are going to work for someone else or serve as a free-lance consultant. Possessing this positive self-concept won't be enough if you really want to make a career, both personally and financially, as a consultant. You must be the kind of person who is highly self-motivated, well organized, and willing to work long hours for limited initial success. After all, what you will be doing is setting up your own small business. We all know the amount of time, energy, and effort it takes to set up and establish a small business, whether it's a neighborhood flower shop or a private consulting firm. We also know that more small businesses fail than succeed. Several colleagues of the authors remain as university professors because they are unwilling to take the risk involved in setting up their own business.

Like the small business entrepreneur, you will need a wide variety of skills that you should assess at the very outset. You will need to know something about running a small business, from the financial side to the personal allocation of time and energy. Being a good presenter or possessing public-speaking skills won't make it in the world of free-lance consulting. Someone has to go out and establish the contacts, sell the business, and follow through with a successful training program. For example, are you willing to go to a company where you have established no prior contacts and talk to them about a training program that they may not perceive as being needed? If you've had any experience in the field of sales, you will be more successful at setting up your own business. If you don't like selling, you may need to think twice about consulting, learn how to sell, or find a partner who is good at selling.

Perhaps the best way to determine whether you have the personal skills necessary for free-lance consulting is to serve as an intern or work for a private consultant. Find someone in your community who has his or her own training company and work for that person for a period of time to see whether this is really something you want to do on your own. If you are still going to school full time, you might check with your department to see if such internships exist so that you can gain that opportunity. Even if they don't have a continuing internship, you can go out and develop one for yourself. This internship experience will prove invaluable when you are ready to go out and set up a business. Trainers should be more than willing to take on a "free" intern even though you are no longer in school.

The second key area that is important for you to assess at the very outset is what you have to offer others by way of training. When time management was first popular, a number of people jumped on the bandwagon and began offering time-management programs for clients. Certainly you can't be successful by going out and offering time management or stress management as your personal skill. We are not saying that you can't work in an area where other consultants already practice, but you do need to find something within your background and/or training that makes you unique as a trainer. This is particularly important for the trainer who wants to offer training without a Ph.D. or advanced graduate work, or has not had a career of five or more years as a successful trainer. If you offer the same services as other trainers you should be the best (at least better than the competition).

We do not believe that there is magic in a Ph.D. We do believe that the Ph.D. has high credibility for many potential clients. It can get you in the door of a company; then your experience with other clients becomes your best motivator. The Ph.D. or terminal degree also proves to the potential client that you have the ability to do research, stick to a task, and complete a rigorous plan of study.

The personal assessment table on the next page gives you an opportunity to fill in the blanks in both categories in terms of personal strengths, as well as skills you would like to offer others. We would encourage you to pause and complete this table to ascertain whether you are ready to go into the field of private consulting.

Once you have determined that you are ready for the world and the world is ready for you as a consultant, you need to take a look at your financial statement and decide whether you have the financial assets necessary to launch your own business. If you have a full- or part-time job, you might ease into the consulting business without a great deal of personal and financial sacrifice. If you don't have a job, you ought to have enough money to see yourself through the initial start-up phase of a consulting business. How long is this initial phase? That totally depends on your drive and your ability to sell the kinds of consulting programs you will be offering. You ought to be prepared for at least a period of three months without income from your consulting business. It will take this long to establish contacts, set up consulting schedules, and offer your initial round of training. Many of our colleagues recommend having at least one year's salary, if not two, set aside to see you through the lean times. We have a colleague who had $10,000 set aside to open her consulting business. She opened an office, got stationery and equipment, and developed a brochure. She advertised her workshops on radio and closed within five weeks. Why? The advertising produced no business and there was not enough funding to sustain her program.

Even having the financial means to last three months or more will not be enough, as you will need to invest funds in various kinds of materials. We will discuss this a little bit later when we talk about what it takes to set up your consulting business.

The final thing you need to do in order to get started is to prepare at least a short-term goal statement. Included in that goal statement should be the answers to the following kinds of questions. The list is not all-inclusive, but certainly reflects some of the key factors you should be considering.

1. Do you want to consult on a full-time or part-time basis?
2. Are you willing to devote a lot of time to travel for your consulting practice?

PERSONAL ASSESSMENT TABLE OF TRAINING SKILLS

Subject Matter	Amount of Time You Can Devote to a Training Session:						
	50+ Hours	40 Hours	16 Hours	8 Hours	3 Hours	1 Hour	30 Minutes
1.							
2.							
3.							
4.							
5.							

3. Do you plan to train alone, do you want to work in partnership, or as part of a larger team?

4. What sort of consulting business do you envision three to five years down the road?

These are but a few of the many questions you should be asking yourself as you get started in your own consulting business.

If you have made it this far, you are probably ready to undertake the first and perhaps most difficult task of all in private practice: finding someone to sell your services to. It won't take long to realize that putting your name in the telephone directory or hanging up your shingle as Jane Doe, Communication Consultant, won't bring the horde of business you had hoped for.

How Do You Find Clients?

We are going to start our discussion on finding clients by turning to the area where we think it's the easiest, and we will end this section with the most difficult client-seeking endeavor: making a cold call to a business or professional organization.

You begin your search for clients right in your own backyard, literally. You should turn to your neighbors, to your colleagues, to those folks who attend the religious and/or civic organizations of your choice. These are all good sources to seek out clients for your consulting business. You may not have discovered, for example, that your neighbor happens to be a pilot for a major airline who could put you in contact with the director of their training program. A member of your own church or synagogue may be a vice-president or middle manager of some organization that could certainly use your skills. If you haven't joined one of the multitude of civic organizations, such as the Chamber of Commerce or a speakers' bureau, it doesn't hurt to belong to these organizations as they, too, provide contacts for potential clients. In other words, you should start with the people who you know best, discuss with them the kind of business you are making available for their respective organizations, and, frankly, ask them to do you a favor and put you in contact with decision makers in their organizations. If it bothers you to "use" your friends for this purpose, your chances for success in private consulting are going to be extremely limited. We even know of colleagues teaching at various universities who take advantage of students and their contacts, even their parents, for potential business. Personally, we would caution you about taking advantage of the student-teacher relationship, should that be your avenue to potential consulting. On the other hand, you can let your own ethics guide you once the student-teacher relationship is over and your former student (or teacher) is willing to discuss with you the various consulting skills you have to offer.

As a transition to other contacts, it is sometimes beneficial to offer friends and neighbors your particular skills as a "freebie" for their civic, religious, or other organization. As we are sure you are aware, most organizations have weekly or monthly meetings, and often seek speakers for these meetings. A good way not only to develop your skills but also to establish contacts in the consulting world is to offer a half-hour training session to the civic or religious group. You can then use that contact to talk about other kinds of training you have available, for which you would naturally charge the client. Every successful private consultant has, at one time or another, offered freebies in order to attract further paid business. You can even donate your training as an item for a civic auction.

In addition to your personal contacts, you should begin thinking about new and varied professional organizations you should belong to. If you are currently teaching or working in some other organization, you probably belong to such groups as the Speech Communication Association, the Society for Professional Engineers, or some other academic or professional group. These organizations are good for your own individual professional growth, but you now must look beyond that in order to establish yourself as a professional free-lance consultant. There are a number of organizations we would suggest you consider joining.

The first and perhaps the most important organization to help you establish a professional network is the American Society for Training and Development (ASTD). This national organization links trainers who work for various businesses and organizations with those who are private, free-lance consultants. This can aid you in at least two ways. First, it will provide you with an opportunity to see what is currently in vogue in the field of training and development. Second, it will connect you with those in-house trainers who, from time to time, need the expertise and training programs offered by a free-lance consultant. Thus, by joining ASTD, you are developing a network both nationally and at your local level to broaden those personal contacts we have already talked about. Yes, you should join the local chapter as well as the national association. If there is no other single organization you can afford to join, ASTD would receive our strongest recommendation. This organization offers you more as a trainer than a professional academic organization that represents your training content.

Depending on the type of consulting you plan to do, you may want to join the National Platform Speakers Association or the National Speakers Association. Both of these groups provide for individual growth of their members, as well as a network for organizations seeking to hire individuals as speakers. You should be aware that both of these groups are designed primarily for the person who wants to serve as a keynote speaker, rather than to provide a week-long, or even day-long, seminar on a particular topic. People like Lee Iacocca and other nationally known speakers benefit from affiliation with this type of group. You can benefit from being a member of these groups because you come in contact with successful national speakers, as well as people who might use your particular skills.

Essentially, then, these are the organizations you can join that will do you the most good professionally as a free-lance consultant. There are a number of other organizations we would also like to suggest, depending on your location and how successful your community is at attracting convention business for various business and professional groups. Should you be in a community that has such services available, we would recommend two other groups you might consider.

First, join the Chamber of Commerce of your own community. This will give you another opportunity to come in contact with the business and civic leaders who might avail themselves of your service. Obviously, if you live in a small town, joining such a chamber could be good for you socially, but it may not provide you with the professional kind of contacts you need.

If you are in a relatively large community or in a location that attracts conventions, you may want to join the local Convention Bureau. This will give you access to the names of organizations, as well as the contact person for the groups, that will be establishing conventions and professional meetings in your own community. The announcements of these meetings go many years—up to a decade or more—in advance, so you have an opportunity to call or write the contact person for a particular group for which you may wish to provide training.

Following our own advice, we noted recently that a national organization was holding a series of training programs around the country, one of which was going to be in our hometown. After a telephone call and a meeting, we provided several days of training for the group, and established training programs in other cities that followed over the succeeding months. Needless to say, one or two such contacts and a series of seminars will more than pay for the fees assessed by the Convention Bureau or Chamber of Commerce.

As we move through the list of suggestions, you will begin to see that the ease in contacting and securing clients lessens. We presented our most viable options first, and as we move through the list the options will become somewhat less viable.

The third way to find a potential client is to check out announcements in your local newspapers for what are traditionally known as "requests for proposals." If you check the classified section of your newspaper, you will find listed from time to time various governmental organizations that are requesting proposals on particular types of training that they need for their organizations. Over the years we have been 50 percent successful in responding to these requests for proposals from various local and state governmental agencies. Needless to say, responding to a request takes time, in that you have to draft a proposal before you can really even be considered by the organization. You might be better off using your personal contacts or your professional affiliations as described earlier, rather than blindly responding to classified ads.

We would, however, suggest that you might use the opportunity of a request for proposal as one to establish contact with the requesting agency. It is beneficial to contact the various agencies and describe to them the kinds of services that you have available. You may not be successful on a specific proposal request, but your materials as well as your name will be on file with the agency. Many times, three, four, five months down the road, a government official may recall that you offer training on a specific topic and give you a call for training in that particular area.

The least successful and the most difficult way to find clients is to make a cold call or send a letter to a business where you have no personal or professional contact. If you choose this direction, it would behoove you to research the business and find out the names of people who are in decision-making positions before you send that letter "to whom it may concern." It is far better and more impressive if you can address your letter specifically to the person who might be in charge of training, rather than to say, "Manager, Human Resources."

You should expand your thinking in this category to go beyond the various businesses, manufacturers, and governmental organizations in your community. We have done a number of training programs for professional organizations like the International Court Reporters Association, the Arizona Bar Association, the American Management Association, and other professional groups. Most every profession holds an annual meeting where either their members or their spouses like to receive some form of continued education. Certainly the kinds of skills you have to offer could fall into this category very nicely.

You should also look to the hotels and large motels that may be in your community, particularly those that offer convention services. We have discovered that the meeting managers at these hotels and motels are constantly asked by professional groups to recommend trainers in a particular topic for their members. If you have established contact with the hotel meeting manager, you may be called upon to provide training for a professional group.

We do not want to leave this discussion of finding clients without highlighting a couple of miscellaneous areas that can prove beneficial at times. We have made contacts with professional organizations simply by using the time spent on airplanes and at cocktail parties to talk a little business. Even if you are on a long flight and don't feel like talking, you might find it beneficial to talk to the people around you about their businesses; it may even lead to a discussion of training needs. Obviously the same goes for parties you may be attending. In both cases, don't make a bore of yourself by constantly discussing what you have to offer. You have to use some moderation in presenting yourself and your services to the public.

In conclusion, we would offer one more word of advice in seeking clients. Once you have offered your first, second, or third training program, make sure you follow up with the participants to determine the long-range effectiveness of your program; we talked about this earlier in the chapter on evaluation. In addition to evaluation, however, use the follow-up as an opportunity to suggest other kinds of training programs that you may have available, as well as to provide business cards or information that the former clients can pass on to their friends. Nothing helps your consulting practice more than a referral by a motivated customer. We find that most of our business comes from the referrals of satisfied clients.

Now that you have begun to find clients and you have decided what it is you are going to offer, you need to consider such things as office space, equipment, and materials. In the next section we will talk about these kinds of needs.

What Office Space and Equipment Do You Need?

The well-equipped office of a private consultant can range from the immaculate top-floor suite of a downtown highrise to an answering service or even an answering machine in one's own home or apartment. The bottom line is having just enough to make your business successful. Though many private consultants start out with a phone answering machine, we would recommend that you begin with an answering service if you cannot afford to have an office and a staff. The answering service will generally provide you with a mailing address and someone to answer the phone on a full-time if not 24-hour basis. Be certain that you shop around before hiring such a service as some are more efficient not only at answering your calls, but also at providing you with a record of all calls that have been received. Ask to see a list of clients that your answering service responds to before you select and finalize a contract. You will want to make certain that they don't answer the phone for another service, or that the location will provide bad publicity because it is also the mail drop for various kinds of unsavory business endeavors. The last thing you want is to see the address of your answering service listed on nationwide television as the mailing point for some kind of TV-advertised product.

We have suggested you use an answering service rather than an answering machine or voicemail because your potential client is leaving a message with a human being. Most people prefer direct contact. An effective answering service can project an image of success, of your being a busy consultant. An answering machine or voicemail, on the other hand, can leave an impression of a less than successful practice. An answering service telling callers that you are not available at the moment is more professional than a taped message saying the caller should leave a name and number at the tone. And if you leave the office and fail to turn on the machine during normal business hours, your image suffers even more. The cost of an answering service will vary, but it is well worth the expense. Make sure that you check out the quality of the service before you make a commitment to a long-term contract. You don't want an inept answering service to say, "Acme Pest Control" when answering your phone call.

As your business begins to increase you will need to consider maintaining some kind of an office. Again, the type of office can vary from a small, shared space to the top-floor suite. Unless you have space dedicated in your home for an office, we would encourage you to find some kind of place where you can go to work and make phone calls. Until the time that your business grows, you could still use the answering service and its address rather than the address of your office. This will give you an opportunity to work in an inexpensive location, be it your home or a shared office space, and still maintain the answering service for the prestige address in a desired location, even though your office may not be there.

Having established an office, we would encourage you to continue meeting potential clients at their locations rather than yours. This serves two purposes for the betterment of your business. First, it shows that you have a true interest in their business, and it gives you firsthand experience in the client's operation. Second, it allows you to have a smaller, less prestigious office in order to keep your overhead low.

Once you have an office, another consideration is whether you need additional space for equipment, supplies, and possibly even for meeting rooms. Frankly, this is an issue you need not address until you have a full-time consulting business and can afford to have such elaborate space. We would certainly recommend that as you begin considering the need for meeting rooms and additional space, you try to find space in the same location as your office. The last thing you want to do is constantly change the address and phone number of your consulting business, as it makes a bad impression.

We do believe that some credibility can be gained by the placement of an office, or even the answering service that you select. If one area of your community is better known for business and professional organizations, you might look to that location for your answering service and ultimate office needs. This will add to your credibility, and will put you in the same environment as your potential clients.

Once you have determined your office and space needs, you need to think about the kinds and types of equipment you will need to operate your business. We suppose it goes without saying that your first priority is a telephone. Beyond the telephone, there are a number of options for equipment you should purchase or at least have at your disposal on a per-use or rental basis. We will discuss these in their order of priority.

If you have read the rest of this book carefully, you will know that the computer ranks highest on our list of equipment needs, whether you are a private entrepreneur or an in-house trainer. Obviously we think the computer is going to become the focal point for the successful trainer. The type and capacity of the computer is both a reflection of your current and future needs and your current financial obligations. As we said in chapter 9, we would encourage you to have more capacity than you feel you currently need so that you can grow into the computer rather than having to replace it because you selected an outdated, obsolete piece of equipment in the first place. Computers are quickly becoming multi-media in their applications. The price of computers is such that you could probably, in today's market, equip yourself with a computer, all of the necessary software, and a printer that would produce letter quality materials for approximately $1500.

Beyond the computer, there are several types of equipment that you should at least have at your disposal. The first we would recommend, again depending on the type of consulting that you plan to do, is a video recorder, monitor, and camera. If you are interested in any aspect of communication as the basis for your training, video equipment will certainly prove to be invaluable. We do not recommend specific equipment, but we would recommend that you look into a VHS system as opposed to some of the others that are available. However, the video market, like the computer market, is undergoing rapid change with the miniaturization of video equipment to the point where we will be using quarter-inch videotape instead of the current half-inch tape. This technology is moving forward in leaps and bounds so the most we can recommend in the area of video is that you consider the state-of-the-art at the time you decide to buy or rent equipment. Keep in mind that within a year or two you may find what you have to be obsolete, but still functional for many years to come.

After video equipment, you should make certain that you have access to a good copy machine. Many potential clients want to receive copies of proposals as well as samples of previous training materials you may have used. As such, you should find a good copy service that is not only reasonable and speedy, but also provides quality copies that will enhance rather than detract from your credibility. Unless you are a full-time, highly successful consultant, you will probably not need to purchase your own copy equipment.

In chapter 8 we talked about the various kinds of audiovisual equipment you can use to enhance your training materials. Like the copy machine, audiotape recorders, overhead projectors, slide projectors, and other such audiovisual materials are things that you could rent rather than purchase. (Probably because at one time or another they were students or had an interest in music, most consultants own their own tape recorders and CD players. You probably fit into this category. You can use them for many training purposes.) Overhead and slide projectors are a bit expensive and you may want to consider either building the rental fee into your training fee, or asking your client to provide such equipment for you. You can use the computer video adapter that we discussed in chapter 8 if the audience is not too large.

There probably is no other equipment that you would need for your consulting business unless, of course, you are doing dictation, in which case you may want to have some kind of dictating machine and playback unit. We believe that after the purchase of a computer or at least the rental of one, most of your capital should be invested in material needs for your business, a topic we would like to discuss next.

What Materials Do You Need?

Essentially there are three items you must have before you even start conversations with the first client. You should have designed and produced a good business card that is coordinated with your stationery. You can design these items yourself or you can hire another entrepreneurial consultant to design your cards and stationery for you. Either way, we would recommend that you find something that is not only unique, but also makes a good, strong, first impression. Stationery that looks like it was designed on a copy machine will certainly not add to your credibility. Remember, your business card and stationery not only help you make that initial impression, but also help form a lasting impression, since they stay behind after the contact.

At some early point in your business, you should design a professional-looking brochure that can be used to advertise your services. We would recommend a brochure that allows for inserts so that as you expand your business and offer new and varied services, you will not have to scrap the initial brochure, but rather can add and delete inserts as your organization changes. To get an idea of what you might do, we would recommend that you check around at various printing houses to see the kinds and varieties of products they have produced. They will also give you some ideas for stationery and business cards.

The next item you need by way of material comes as your business begins to grow. We suggest that you keep on file a portfolio of programs and letters of response to your programs. Many new clients want to know how others have responded to your training, so if you have letters on file in a portfolio, it is an easy task to show them these evaluations. You should also keep copies of any news releases and other publicity materials in that portfolio.

The last material need we have hinted at earlier when we asked you to make a personal assessment of finance. To say that you will need cash, and lots of it, may be an understatement. Once you have provided financially to live for a period of two, three, or four months, you will need an additional cash supply of $1,000 or more to provide for stationery, brochures, business cards, computer, and office-related needs. It doesn't take long before that $1,000 becomes

$2,000, $3,000, or as much as $10,000 to get your business off the ground. A bare-bones budget of at least $ 1,000 will be necessary to cover answering service, computer (partial payment), and material needs.

Now that you have established your business and begun to look for clients, one of the first questions you ask yourself and in this case are asking us, is "Do you advertise and, if so, how?" We would answer the first question by saying that it is totally up to you. To advertise or not advertise is largely a function of the services you have to offer. We are going to make some suggestions, though, that allow you to advertise without paying for a display ad in the local newspaper. We think that these forms of advertising will do you more good in the long run than putting down a large chunk of money for a straight commercial ad in a newspaper or magazine. What are they?

One of the best forms of advertising is to get your name in the newspaper as often as possible. No, we are not suggesting you rob a bank or steal a car; rather, you should be submitting articles to the newspaper, as well as contacting the feature editor for special stories. You should plan short articles that offer perhaps a unique perspective on some of the national events in your specialty or special-interest articles on your specialty in a given population. For example, if you are interested in promoting workshops and training programs in interpersonal communication, you might call up the feature editor and propose a story on interpersonal communication and the increasing crisis of suicide. The feature-article writer would then interview you on a story relating interpersonal communication and suicide.

As a parallel, you should look into appearances on local radio and television talk shows. Many larger communities have stations whose format is devoted to evening talk shows that are constantly looking for people to appear as guests. Develop a list of topics you are interested in talking about and submit this to the producers of the various talk shows so that they might schedule appearances. You will be surprised the number of clients you can pick up from appearances on radio, television, and even in the newspaper.

Aside from these free forms of advertising, you can also use brochures and special-interest fliers to spread the word on your services. We strongly urge that brochures and fliers be made available to trainees at the end of each and every workshop so that the trainee and the flier can serve as advertising for your services.

In essence we are saying that you really don't have to pay to advertise if you take advantage of the media that are at your disposal in your community. Media look for stories and, with a little creativity on your part, you can provide the stories and at the same time gain free publicity, which can be turned into contacts with potential clients.

How Much Do You Charge?

Unless you have had some experience working with a consultant or have had contact with those who are doing consulting, the biggest question you have in mind is how much to charge. Our off-the-cuff response is that you charge all the market will bear, but that may be a bit facetious. We stressed in chapter 4 the need to do a needs assessment before providing training, and we would encourage you to take that same advice before deciding how much you should charge for your services. There are a number of factors you should keep in mind as you begin to develop some kind of flexible pricing structure.

The most important consideration is that you want to be competitive with other consultants in your marketplace. If you provide services and your price is much lower than your competitors, you will be viewed as perhaps not as credible as those around you. Some potential clients will feel that if your prices are that low, you can't be that good. At the other end of the continuum, you shouldn't charge too much. Word spreads quickly among potential clients if you are overcharging, particularly if you are not offering full value for the money.

Where does that leave you with regard to pricing? The best we can do is to give you a range of what private consultants are charging. This range goes from a low of $100 to $200 a day to as high as $5,000 to $10,000 a day. Those at the upper end of the continuum are obviously nationally known, highly in demand consultants who are probably worth every penny of the $10,000. Those at the low end of the continuum are those with little experience and perhaps new to the market. Where you price yourself should fall somewhere in between.

One way to determine a fair market value is to look to the charges paid to other professionals, such as accountants and lawyers. Using an hourly fee charged by other professionals gives you a benchmark.

There are other factors in addition to what others are charging and what you are worth that should go into your pricing policy. We have always felt that you need to calculate the amount of preparation time, the amount of materials that you are going to have to pay for, and the length of your training program into your ultimate pricing structure. In other words, we might charge a client less for a training program if we know and can be somewhat assured that we will be doing a whole series of training programs for that client, rather than just a one-shot training package. We will also take into consideration the amount of travel time to and from the consultation as a part of our fee. Some private consultants charge the same price on a daily basis, whether they are training or traveling. You will have to be flexible and test out the marketplace on this issue.

You now have enough information to go out and establish your own consulting firm. The only other question you might want to consider is whether or not you work alone or team up with one or more individuals. Our preference is to have a loose collection of individuals, all of whom can work alone or as part of a team. Since we come from an academic environment, we find the intellectual stimulation of working with others to be quite useful in the development of training ideas and workshop designs. You are the best judge of how well you can work alone or with others, but there is at least one additional advantage to being part of a loose-knit team. As an individual, there are only certain topic areas in which you are qualified to consult. You will undoubtedly come across a client who may express initial interest in something that you do very effectively, only to discover after the needs assessment the client really needs training in some area outside of your specialty. By being part of a team, you can suggest how your group or other members of your group can meet the need for the client. This keeps you in good contact with the client should further consultation be necessary in your area of expertise. This also prevents you from spreading yourself too thin by saying, "Sure, we can do training in that area. What would you like?"

The last major issue we would like to consider is whether you incorporate your business. This is a question that only your tax accountant and attorney can answer with any finality. For the most part, we would recommend that you start out your business on what is considered a Schedule C for your tax purposes and then modify your operation depending on how large your consulting practice grows. In the beginning you probably do not need to file for incorporation, but as you add employees and increase the size of your budget, you will have to consider a potential incorporation. Incorporating is a big step, and it can cost you from $500 to as much as $2000 or more just for the initial incorporation papers. It will also require further support from clerical staff and even your tax accountant to provide quarterly returns for the corporation. All we can suggest is that you look into the matter of incorporation, but work out any details with a tax consultant.

Pitfalls and Positives

In case you get the idea that private consulting is a glamorous, fun-filled, exciting career, we should talk a little bit about the other side so that you approach private consulting aware of all the problems you can face. The examples and points that we are going to make in this section are based upon our conversations with those who have gone the private consulting route, some of whom have returned to the more stable environment of in-house training or college or university teaching.

Most important, the world of consulting is hard work, long hours, and occasionally boring. As a first-time, full-time consultant, you may spend days making contacts trying to find that first client. Once the clients begin to emerge, you may find presenting the same old workshop on stress management to be as boring and repetitious as the job you left for consulting. We know many consultants who spend day after day, week after week doing the same type of workshop for different groups for as little as $200 a day, simply to be able to pay the rent and expenses. We know those are not the ones you read about, but they are the reality of private consulting. As with professional athletes, not every consultant brings in over a million dollars a year in business.

Another pitfall of the private consultant is that you may find yourself being pulled in a variety of directions simply to survive. Suppose you have just completed your first successful training contract on listening skills for a client and he or she asks if you also could provide training in public speaking. You may find yourself saying that you can do it. Pretty soon you may find yourself offering training in thirty different topics because you once needed the money to survive. Unless you are a super trainer, you will find yourself spread too thin to be credible in the eyes of clients. We recommend you focus your business on your area of expertise and tell your clients that you know other consultants who can help them. You maintain your credibility and respect in the eyes of clients, and you build a support network among other consultants who may return the favor. While you may lose an immediate training program, you will gain in the long run.

Another problem faced by private consultants is the amount of time spent traveling. It's been said that it's hard to be an expert in your own hometown. As such, you may spend hours on the road, traveling to cities far and wide to present your material, because you have not been recognized in your own community. To avoid this pitfall, you should find ways to make your travel time as productive as possible. Nevertheless, one can quickly tire of plane flights, hotel rooms, and eating meals on the road.

In case you are still determined to set out as a private consultant on a full- or part-time basis, we will conclude by looking at the positive side of the picture. There are some advantages to approaching training on a full-time, entrepreneurial basis.

Perhaps the greatest advantage is that you are the master of your own destiny. Like the small business concern, you can make or break the company on the basis of your sole efforts. If you are successful, you owe it to yourself; if you are a failure, you can take the blame. Of course, being an optimist and making it this far, you should be nothing but successful.

Being a consultant allows you to choose the kinds of clients and locations that you want. Probably we would encourage you to select only a few categories of clients or types of training programs; being a private consultant allows you that freedom. You may choose to work only with health-related professionals, rather than every type of company that exists. You may also choose to provide training only in the area of presentation skills and not be concerned so much about the type of clients that you work with. As a consultant, you can make these choices for yourself.

For some, travel, eating out, and staying in hotels can be a pitfall; for others, this can be a real thrill and challenge. If you like that kind of life, private consulting can offer you that opportunity.

So if you have got an idea, if you like to sell, if you know how to market yourself, and if you have a financial basis from which to work for several months, then go out and take up private consulting and see how successful you can be. Like most things, if you don't try it, it will always look like a better opportunity than it may really be. So, as we said in the beginning, start with an internship or work for a consultant, and then move gradually into the world of private consulting. Good luck.

Bibliography

American Society for Training and Development. (1976). *Training and development handbook: A guide to human resource development* (2nd ed.). New York: McGraw-Hill.

American Society for Training and Development. (1982). *Compensation in human resource development*. Baltimore: ASTD Publishing Services.

Anderson, R. E., & Kasl, E. S. (1982). *The costs and financing of adult education and training*. Lexington, MA: Lexington Books.

Aslanian, C., & Brickell, H. (1980). *Americans in transition: Life changes as reasons for adult learning*. New York: College Entrance Examination Board.

Baird, L., Schneier, C. E., & Laird, D. (1983). *The training and development sourcebook*. Amherst, MA: Human Resource Development Press.

Babbie, E. R. (1985). *The practice of social research* (4th ed.). Belmont, CA: Wadsworth.

Bell, C., & Margolis, F. (1982). *A presenter's guide to conferences*. Baltimore: ASTD Publishing Services.

Bellman, G. (1990). *The consultant's calling: Bringing who you are to what you do*. New York: Jossey-Bass.

Bellman, G. (1992). *Getting things done when you are not in charge*. New York: Berrett-Koehler.

Benne, K. D., & Sheats, P. (1948). Functional roles of group members. The *Journal of Social Science*, Spring, 41–49.

Blake, R. (1984). *Synergogy.* San Francisco: Jossey-Bass.

Blake, R., & Mouton, J. S. (1978). *The new managerial grid.* Houston: Gulf.

Blake, R., & Mouton, J. S. (1982). How to choose a leadership style. *Training and Development Journal* 36(2), 39–46.

Blank, W. E. (1983). *Handbook for developing competency-based training programs.* Englewood Cliffs, NJ: Prentice-Hall.

Block, P. (1981). *Flawless consulting.* Austin, TX: Learning Concepts.

Bridges, W. (1994). *Job shift.* New York: Addison-Wesley.

Brookfield, S. (1986). *Understanding and facilitating adult learning.* San Francisco: Jossey-Bass.

Burrus, Daniel, & Gittines, Roger. (1994). *Technotrends: 24 Technologies that will revolutionize our lives.* New York: HarperCollins.

Camp, R. R., Blanchard, P. N., & Huszczo, G. E. (1986). *Toward a more organizationally effective training strategy and practice.* Englewood Cliffs, NJ: Prentice-Hall.

Carnevale, A. (1983). *Human capital: A high-yield corporate investment.* Baltimore: ASTD Publishing Services.

Carr, David, & Johansson, Henry. (1994). *Best practices in reengineering: What works and what doesn't in the reengineering process.* New York: McGraw-Hill.

Chalofsky, N., & Lincoln, C. I. (1983). *Up the HRD ladder.* Reading, MA: Addison-Wesley.

Champy, James. (1994). *Reengineering management: The mandate for new leadership.* New York: HarperCollins.

Covey, Steven C., et al. (1994). *First things first.* New York: Simon & Schuster.

Craig, R. L. (ed.). (1987). *Training and development handbook* (2nd ed.). New York: McGraw-Hill.

Cross, K. P. (1976). *Accent on learning.* San Francisco: Jossey-Bass.

Cross, K. P. (1979). *Lifelong learning: Purposes and priorities.* Long Beach, CA: Council for the Advancement of Experiential Learning.

Cross, K. P. (1981). *Adults as learners.* San Francisco: Jossey-Bass.

Culbert, S. A., & McDonough, J. (1980). *The invisible war: Pursuing self-interests at work.* New York: Wiley.

Daniels, W. R. 1995. *Breakthrough performance.* Mill Valley, CA: ACT Publishing.

Davies, I. K. (1980). *Instructional techniques.* New York: McGraw-Hill.

Davis, L. N., & McCallon, E. (1974). *Planning, conducting, and evaluating workshops.* Austin, TX: Learning Concepts.

Deal, T. E., & Kennedy, R. A. (1982). *Corporate cultures: The rites and rituals of corporate life.* Reading, MA: Addison-Wesley.

Desatnick, R. (1980). *The business of human resource management.* New York: Wiley.

Donaldson, L., & Scannell, E. (1979). *Human resource development: The new trainer's guide.* Reading, MA: Addison-Wesley.

Edelman, Joel, & Crain, Mary Beth. (1994). *Tao of negotiation: How you can prevent, resolve and transcend conflict in work and everyday life.* New York: HarperCollins.

Fetteroll, E., Nadler, L., & Nadler, L. (1986). *The trainer's resource: Comprehensive guide to packaged training programs.* Amherst, MA: Human Resource Development Press.

Fournies, F. F. (1982). *Coaching for improved work performance.* Baltimore: ASTD Publishing Services.

Friedman, P. G., & Yarbrough, E. A. (1985). *Training strategies from start to finish.* Englewood Cliffs, NJ: Prentice-Hall.

Galbraith, John Kenneth. (1994). *A short history of financial euphoria.* New York: Penguin

Garfield, Charles. (1994). *Second to none: The productive power of putting people first.* New York: Avon

Garry, W. (ed.). (1982). *A checklist for technical skills and other training.* Baltimore: ASTD Publishing Services.

Gaw, B. (1979). Processing questions: An aid to completing the learning cycle. *1979 annual handbook for group facilitators* (pp. 147–152). La Jolla, CA: University Associates.

Gilbert, T. F. (1982). *Human competence.* New York: McGraw-Hill.

Goldstein, K. M., & Blackman, S. (1978). *Cognitive style: Five approaches and relevant research.* New York: Wiley.

Gray, John. (1992). *Men are from mars—women are from venus.* New York: HarperCollins.

Gross, R. (1977). *The lifelong learner.* New York: Simon & Schuster.

Guild, P. B. (1983). How to involve learners in your lectures. *Training,* April, 43–45.

Hackman, R. C. (1909). *The motivated working adult.* New York: American Management Association.

Hamel, Gary, & Prahalad, C. K. (1994). *Competing for the future.* Boston: Harvard Business.

Hammer, Michael, and Champy, James. (1993). *Reengineering the corporation.* New York: HarperCollins.

Harrington, James H. (1994). *Total improvement management: Creating the custom-tailored turnaround.* New York: McGraw-Hill.

Harrison, M. I. (1986). *Diagnosing organizations: Methods, models, and processes.* Newbury Park, CA: Sage.

Hart, L. B. (1982). *Learning from conflict: A handbook for trainers and group leaders.* Reading, MA: Addison-Wesley.

Hayes, W. G., & Williams, E. I. (1971). Supervisory training—an index of change. *Training and Development Journal* 25(4), 34–38.

Heil, Gary, Tate, Rick, & Parker, Tom. (1994). *Leadership and the customer revolution: Making the rhetoric of change a reality.* New York: Van Nostrand Reinhold.

Hersey, P., & Blanchard, K. H. (1982a). Leadership style: Attitudes and behaviors. *Training and Development Journal* 36(5), 50–53.

Hersey, P., & Blanchard, K. H. (1982b). *Management of organizational behavior: Utilizing human resources* (4th ed.). Englewood Cliffs, NJ: Prentice-Hall.

Ingalls, J. (1973). *A trainer's guide to andragogy* (rev. ed.). Washington, DC: U.S. Government Printing Office (HCFA–73–05–301).

Jamieson, D. (1982). Development in an era of paradigm shifts, changing boundaries and personal challenge—a dialogue with Robert Tannenbaum. *Training and Development Journal* 36(4), 34.

Johansen, Robert, & Swigart, Rob. (1994). *Upsizing the individual in the downsized organization.* New York: Addison-Wesley.

Keil, E. C. (1982). *Assessment centers: A guide for human resources management.* Reading, MA: Addison-Wesley.

Kirkpatrick, D. L. (1982). *Evaluating training programs.* Baltimore: ASTD Publishing Services.

Knowles, M. S. (1980). *The modern practice of adult education* (2nd ed.). New York: Cambridge Books.

Knowles, M. S. (1984a). *The adult learner: A neglected species* (3rd ed.). Houston: Gulf.

Knowles, M. S. (1984). *Andragogy in action.* San Francisco: Jossey-Bass.

Knox, A. B. (1977). *Adult development and learning.* San Francisco: Jossey-Bass.

Korman, A. K. (1977). *Organizational behavior.* Englewood Cliffs, NJ: Prentice-Hall.

Kostick, N. M., & Pearse, R. (1977). The dynamics of productive compatibility. *Management Review* 66, 18–54.

Kramlinger, T., & Zemke, R. (1982). *Figuring things out: A trainer's guide.* Reading, MA: Addison-Wesley.

Kuhn, S. (1970). *The structure of scientific revolutions* (2nd ed.). Chicago: University of Chicago Press.

Laird, D. (1982). *Approaches to training and development.* Reading, MA: Addison-Wesley.

Landrum, Gene H. (1994). *Profiles of female genius: Thirteen creative women who changed the world.* New York: Prometheus Books.

Leach, J. J. (1979). Organization needs analysis: A new methodology. *Training and Development Journal* 33, September, 66–69.

Loden, M., & Rosener, J. B. (1991). *Workforce America!* Homewood, IL: Business One-Irwin.

Loughary, J. W., & Hopson, B. (1979). *Producing workshops, seminars, and short courses: A trainer's handbook.* Chicago: Association Press/Follett.

Mager, R. F., & Pipe, P. (1970). *Analyzing performance problems.* Belmont, CA: Fearon Publishers.

McKillip, J. (1986). *Need analysis: Tools for the human services and education.* Newbury Park, CA: Sage.

Mears, Peters. (1994). *Quality improvement—tools and techniques.* New York: McGraw-Hill

Metzger, Robert O. (1993). *Developing a consulting practice.* Newbury Park, CA: Sage.

Michalak, D. F., & Yager, E. G. (1980). *Making the training process work.* New York: Harper & Row.

Morris, Daniel C., & Brandon, Joel S. (1994). *Re-engineering your business.* New York: McGraw-Hill.

Nadler, L. (1982a). *Corporate human resources development: A management tool.* Baltimore: ASTD Publishing Services.

Nadler, L. (1982b). *The critical events model: For designing training programs.* Reading, MA: Addison-Wesley.

Nadler, L. (1982c). *The trainer's resource.* Amherst, MA: Human Resource Development Press.

Nadler, L. (1984). *Handbook for human resource development.* New York: Wiley.

Nagel, Roger N., Goldman, Steven L., & Preiss, Kenneth. (1994). *Agile competitors and virtual organizations: Strategies for winning in the 21st century.* New York: VANS.

Naisbitt, J. (1982). *Megatrends.* New York: Warner.

Newstrom, J. W. (1980). Evaluating the effectiveness of training methods. *Personnel Administrator* 25, 55–60.

Newstrom, J. W., and Lilyquist, J. M. (1979). Selecting needs analysis methods. *Training and Development Journal,* October, 52–56.

Newstrom, J. W., & Scannell, E. (1982). *Games trainers play: Experiential learning exercises.* New York: McGraw-Hill.

Oakley, Ed, & Krug, Doug. (1994) *Enlightened leadership: Getting to the heart of change.* New York: Fireside.

Orsburn, J. D., Moran, L., Musselwhite, E., & Zenger, J. H. (1990). *Self-directed work teams.* Homewood, IL: Business One-Irwin.

O'Toole, J. (1986). *Vanguard management: Redesigning the corporate future.* Garden City, NY: Doubleday.

Patton, M. Q. (1978). *Utilization-focused evaluation.* Beverly Hills: Sage Publications.

Peters, T. J., & Waterman, R. H., Jr. (1982). *In search of excellence.* New York: Harper & Row.

Pfeiffer, J. W., & Jones, J. G. (eds.). (1969–1980). *Handbook of structured experiences for human relations training* (Vols. I–IX). San Diego: University Associates.

Professional Development Committee, Ontario Society for Training and Development. (1982). *Competency analysis for trainers: A personal planning guide.*

Reierson, L., & Walsh, M. (1994). *Teamwork breakthrough: Managing one level up.* Monterey: Saltwater Institute.

Ribler, R. (1983). *Training development guide.* Reston, VA: Reston Publishing.

Rifkin, Jeremy. (1994). *End of work: The decline of the global labor force and the dawn of the post-market era.* New York: Tarcher.

Rogers, C. R. (1969). *Freedom to learn.* Columbus, OH: Charles E. Merrill.

Rosenbaum, L., & Dresner, B. (1979). Abolishing boredom on the job. *Canadian Business* 52(6), 66–73.

Rudolph, E. E., & Johnson, B. R. (1983). *Communication consulting: Another teaching option.* Urbana, IL: Eric Clearinghouse on Reading and Communication Skills.

Scannell, E. (1982). *Supervisory communications.* Dubuque, IA: Kendall-Hunt.

Schein, V. E. (1971). An evaluation of a long-term management training program. *Training and Development Journal* 25(12), 28–34.

Shonk, J. (1992). *Team-based organizations.* Homewood, IL: Business One-Irwin.

Tannen, Deborah. (1986). *That's not what I meant.* New York: Ballentine Books.

Tannen, Deborah. (1990). *You just don't understand.* New York: Morrow.

Tannen, Deborah. (1994). *Talking from 9-5.* New York: Morrow.

Taylor, C. (1991). *The ethics of authenticity.* Cambridge: Harvard University Press.

Thayer, R. (1990). How I learned to let my workers lead. *Harvard Business Review* 68(6).

Tough, A. (1967). *Learning without a teacher.* Toronto: Ontario Institute for Studies in Education.

Tough, A. (1979). *The adult's learning projects* (2nd ed.). Toronto: Ontario Institute for Studies in Education.

Ulschak, F. (1983). *Human resource development.* Reston, VA: Reston Publishing.

Valenzi, E., & Dessler, G. (1978). Relationships of leader behavior, subordinate role ambiguity, and subordinate job satisfaction. *Academy of Management Journal* 21, 671–678.

Van de Ven, A. H., & Delbecq, A. L. (1971). Nominal versus interacting group processes for committee decision-making effectiveness. *Academy of Management Journal,* June, 203–212.

Verduin, J., Miller, H., & Greer, C. (1978). *Adults teaching adults.* Austin: Learning Concepts.

Wexley, K. N., & Latham, G. P. (1981). *Developing and training human resources in organizations.* Glenview, IL: Scott-Foresman.

Wilber, K. (1981). *Up from Eden: A transpersonal view of human evolution.* Garden City, NY: Anchor Press/Doubleday.

Williams, F., & Dordick, H. S. (1983). *The executive's guide to information technology.* New York: Wiley.

Wurman, Richard S. (1989). *Information anxiety.* New York: Bantam.

Wurman, Richard S. (1992). *Follow the yellow brick road.* New York: Bantam.

Index